*The*
# SECRET TO
# ATTRACTING
# MONEY

## ALSO BY DR. JOE VITALE

*Faith*

*Expect Miracles*

*Zero Limits*

*The Fifth Phrase*

*The Miracle*

*The Art and Science of Results*

*The*

# SECRET TO ATTRACTING MONEY

## A PRACTICAL SPIRITUAL SYSTEM FOR ABUNDANCE AND PROSPERITY

# DR. JOE VITALE

**MEDIA**

Published 2020 by Gildan Media LLC
aka G&D Media
www.GandDmedia.com

Front cover design by Tom McKeveny

Interior design by Meghan Day Healey of Story Horse, LLC

Library of Congress Cataloging-in-Publication Data is available upon
request

ISBN: 978-1-7225-0545-5

10   9   8   7   6   5   4   3   2   1

# CONTENTS

# FOREWORD

Would you like to attract more money into your life? Of course you would. That's a simple question to answer, but did you realize the solution may be just as simple? Regardless of the state of the economy or anything else going on, the answer lies within you. It's simply a matter of removing the blocks that prevent you from attracting money—and lots of it.

In this powerful new book, Dr. Joe Vitale blends the best of the practical and the spiritual to reveal a new system for attracting money that will show you how to uncover and get rid of the programming that is creating lack in your life. He'll also show how to rewrite this programming to attract riches.

Based on spiritual principles that work in the material world, Joe's compelling book will teach you how to easily attract money in a healthy, happy, and easy way. Joe will teach you how to build a business that fits your ultimate purpose; he'll also reveal a revolutionary and powerful new concept in marketing.

Whether you're a longtime follower of Joe's or are being introduced to him for the first time, you are in for a treat as Joe teaches you the secret to attracting money as only he can.

# ONE
## SEVEN KEY POINTS
## ABOUT MONEY

The secret to attracting money is different from anything you've ever heard before. Certainly there are books out there that talk about investments, real estate, and ways to balance the financial numbers. That's not this book. There are books that talk about the spiritual side of money. That's also not this book. This book combines the practical and the spiritual to help you attract money easily and effortlessly.

I know that this works, because I've been doing it for myself for over thirty years. At one point in my life, I was homeless; from there, I went to poverty; from there, I went to scrambling and struggling; from there, I went to thriving; and from there, I went to a level of abundance, prosperity, and luxury that would be hard for most people to even imagine.

So how does somebody go from homeless man to best-selling author and multimillionaire? Somebody who has appeared in numerous movies and TV shows, and has audio products, DVD products, and a wealth of other resources that people are learning from?

It happens from knowing the secret to attracting money. That's what I'm going to reveal here. I've gone from being an unknown to author of over thirty books. I've produced and profited from a lot of material, and I've done it by knowing the secret to attracting money.

Years ago, when I was homeless on the streets in Dallas, I had no clue how to attract money. I did have a desire. I did want to be an author. I wanted to write books that would inspire people and make a difference in their lives. I had a noble goal (as you may have), but I didn't know how to attract the money to make it happen.

I had to learn the hard way. I had to work on myself. I had to read the different books that were out there and develop my own inside out approach to attracting money. As I have, life has become a moment by moment experience of wonder, amazement, and awe.

All of this is available to you as well. With this book, you're getting thirty years of distilled wisdom, from which you will reap the benefits.

I need you to be aware of something: your mindset. As you read this book, your mind is going to be judging it, me, and all the concepts and secrets that I share with you. You want to be aware of this, because this is part of the secret to attracting money. Most of us have a negative mindset: we look at things with an expectation for things *not* to work out. So I'm going to invite you to play a game called "What if Up?" which was created by Mendhi Audlin.

Most of our mental processing goes, "What if down?" For example, as you're reading this book, you might be thinking, "What if this book is terrible? What if Joe doesn't give me the information I need? What if this doesn't really help me attract money? What if this becomes a waste of time, a waste of money, a waste of my investment and my energy? What if it doesn't work?"

That's "What if down?" thinking. It will make your mind go in a negative direction, and you will actually find reasons for the program not to work.

The "What if Up?" game goes in the opposite direction. Instead you ask questions such as, "What if this is the book that finally changes my life? What if this is the book that truly helps me attract money? What if this is the book that gets me out of debt? What if this is the book that helps me become financially free? What if this is the book that I rave about, that I keep reading over and over again, because it makes me feel so fantastic? What if this book becomes the greatest investment in my life?"

Notice how you feel. You are probably more excited just from playing this game in your own head. This is part of what I need to teach you, because the secret to attracting money has a lot to do with the inside of you rather than the outside. Too many people give their power away to the economy, to their jobs, to whatever the media is telling them. But the real power is in you. It's in your mindset.

By playing "What if Up?", which is a positive way of directing your mind, you start to expect something different. You start to expect that this book is going to give you all the information you need to attract money easily and effortlessly, beginning today, beginning now.

When you have an expectation, you turn on your mental radar to find all the information, all the facts, to support that belief. If you expect something *not* to work out, you will look around and find all the evidence for it not to work out. Your expectation is actually creating your reality.

It all comes down to your mindset. I'm inviting you to have a mindset of success. I'm inviting you to have the mindset that these secrets will change your relationship to money so that you can attract it right now. This is your wake-up call. This is the Holy Grail you've been looking for. This is the information that will actually pump money into your life by removing all the inner blocks that have been blocking it from coming to you.

Why should you be reading this book right now? First of all, if you look at history, you're going to see that there have always been recessions, depressions, times of struggle. If you look at the history of any country, you find that there's an ebb and flow to it; at times its people experience prosperity, but at other times they experience the reverse.

You can get caught up in this thinking if you're not awake and aware. I want you to be awake and aware. I want you to be alert to the idea that your power source is actually within you. It's not in the media, it's not in the economy, it's not outside at all. When you become aware of this fact, you can become immune to what's going on in the outer world. You can actually find financial security.

Even in times such as the Great Depression in the 1930s, some people became millionaires. When some people were standing in soup lines or ending their lives, others were finding opportunities and becoming very wealthy. Some of the greatest millionaires have been created during a depression.

Outer circumstances do not dictate what's going on in your life. You are the one that's in control. But up to now, you have not been consciously in control of that inner reality in order to attract money. I know that first-hand, because when I was on the streets in Dallas and later, when I was in poverty in Houston, I was certainly not awake to the idea that I was the one that was not attracting money, I was the one that was attracting my struggle, poverty, and homelessness.

If you've seen the movie *The Secret* (in which I appeared), read some of my other books, or listened to one of my audio programs such as *The Missing Secret,* you may remember that I have spoken about the *law of attraction*. The law of attraction causes you to attract, or not attract, the money that you would like to have in your life. The law of attraction says that everything you get in your life is due to your mental processes. It's due to your thoughts. It's due to your beliefs.

It's not enough to understand the law of attraction on a superficial level in order to attract money. You have to know another law: the *law of right action.*

That's why this book is different from the others. I'm going to explain the law of attraction, so you can get it to work for you to attract money. I'm also going to explain the law of right action, because movement is also required to get money to circulate into your life. You need to know both laws to make this happen.

Let's quickly look into the law of attraction, which says that everything you have coming into your life is based on your beliefs. The deeper aspect of this law is the fact that beliefs are unconscious. For the most part, it's not what you are *consciously* thinking but what you are *unconsciously* thinking about money that causes you to attract or not attract it.

If you want to know what you unconsciously think about money, look around. Do you have money? If you do and you're happy with that abundance right now, then you have beliefs that support you in attracting money. If you're looking around and saying to yourself, "I don't have money. I can't pay my bills. I don't know where the rent check is going to come from. I need to get a job, or I need to get another job," you have beliefs that are not supporting you in attracting money.

In this book, I will help you find the beliefs that are stopping you from attracting money. I will help you release those beliefs and install new ones that will cause you to attract it easily and effortlessly.

If you're interested in getting out of debt, read this book. If want to weather any financial storm that the media may reporting on, read this book. If you want to experience financial freedom and independence, this is the book for you. If you want to want to learn practical, tried, and tested marketing, time management, publicity, organization, and Internet tools that can immediately apply to your business, this is the book for you. If you want to have the time and money to contribute to worthwhile causes that fill your heart with joy, read this book. If you want to attract the career that you are passionate about, read this book. If you want to surrender control and reap the financial rewards that flow naturally when you know the secret to attracting money, read this book. If you want to know how to attract health, a spouse, wealth, even world peace—anything that you can name or imagine—read this book.

*The Secret to Attracting Money* reveals a practical and also spiritual system for abundance and prosperity. As I've said, this program has definitely worked for me. I've developed all the steps, insights, and methods you'll been reading about here. They have worked to take me from homelessness to celebrity status and great financial rewards.

I'm not the only person that has benefited from these insights. I will be telling you stories of people who have gone from nothing to becoming financially free. They had no idea how to create a product or service, but went on to create one. These are people just like you and me: at one point they were wondering, "How can I achieve financial freedom?"

In addition to being a best-selling author, I've been a business and marketing expert over the last few decades. I'm an Internet marketing, copywriter, publicist, and strategist. I've created new ways of doing marketing online. I've created concepts like hypnotic marketing, hypnotic writing, and hypnotic publicity; I have books out on most of these subjects. I've written a book on the business secrets of the great nineteenth-century showman P. T. Barnum, called *There's a Customer Born Every Minute*. I'm also the creator of the best-selling audio program *The*

*Power of Outrageous Marketing.* It's helped hundreds if not thousands of people.

This book will incorporate both sides of my interests: my spiritual side, the part of me that is interested in the law of attraction, and the marketing side, the part that is interested in the law of right action. Blending both of these causes you to become a money magnet.

## SEVEN KEY POINTS ABOUT MONEY

I want to begin by talking about the seven key points about money that I've discovered.

1. You are totally responsible for the financial experiences that you have in your life. You aren't to blame for them; it's not your fault, but it *is* your responsibility.

2. You are unconsciously absorbing beliefs about money from the culture itself.

3. You are not ruler of the earth, you are not God, but you have far more power, financially and otherwise, than you've ever realized.

4. You can change your thoughts about your money. You need to become aware.

5. You can do the impossible financially.

6. Whatever abundance image you add emotion to will tend to manifest.

7. You can have money miracles happen in your life when you let go of attachment and need.

The first point: you are totally responsible for the financial experiences that you have in your life. You aren't to blame, it's not your fault, but it is your responsibility. This may be a big principle to grasp the first time you encounter it. I know that if somebody went back in a time machine, found me on the streets in Dallas, and said to me, "Joe, you're homeless because of your own beliefs. It's not your fault that you're here, but it is your responsibility," I'd probably have hit him in the mouth, because at that point in time I was into survival. So if you're feeling, "Oh, it's not your fault. It's everybody else's fault," you're going to have to take a deep breath and realize that on an unconscious level, you've been sending out beliefs and energy that are causing you to get the results you have. This is why you are attracting, or not attracting, money. It's based on your unconscious mindset.

Don't worry; this is just a wake-up call. I will explain this principle, I will help you understand it, and I will help you release any blocks within you. But do grasp this first key point: you are totally responsible for where you are financially.

When you own this responsibility, you reclaim your power, and that's essential for understanding how to attract money. You need your inner power to do it. If you've been giving your power away to a job, the government, the media, or anybody that's been causing you to fear, you don't have the internal power you need to attract money. You are responsible, but that's OK. It's not your fault, but it is your responsibility.

The second key point: you have been unconsciously absorbing beliefs about money from the culture—the media, the government, religion, and the school system. Starting from the time you were born, you have been, readily and vulnerably and without question, downloading information about how the world works. When it comes to money, most people believe there's not enough to go around. Most people believe money is evil. Most people believe that wealthy people are greedy, evil, or manipulative.

You have been downloading *beliefs* about money— not facts or reality about money, but beliefs. If these beliefs don't serve you, you will push money away. You'll look around and wonder, "Why don't I have money in my life?" One reason is that you've absorbed limiting, negative beliefs about money from the culture you're in.

Again, this is not bad or negative. It is an opportunity to awaken, and that will happen as you read this book.

You've also absorbed beliefs from your family, from your friends, from your neighborhood. Again, you weren't thinking about it. You probably felt that it was just reality. But these people were sharing beliefs about money with you that became a belief system *in you*. You have to change that in order attract money into your life easily. You'll learn how to do this in this book.

The third point: you are the not ruler of the earth, you are not God, but you have far more financial power than you realize. Most people don't realize that they have more ability, talent, creativity, and inner power to get things done than they imagine. Most people don't try. They don't try to open a new business. They don't try to act on an idea. They don't try to write the book they've been talking about. They don't try, because they don't believe it's possible for them.

I'm not encouraging you to go on an ego trip and think that you rule the earth. But I am encouraging you to dissolve your inner limitations about what's possible for you. You can have more money than you ever thought possible.

You may have to take this in baby steps. When I was homeless, it would be very difficult to imagine becoming a millionaire. But I could imagine bringing in hundreds if not thousands of dollars. As I started to stretch myself and feel more power financially, I could extend what I would welcome into my life. I'm encouraging you to allow yourself to want more, to deserve more, and to expect more. You can have more than you ever thought possible, because you have more power, financially and otherwise, within your own body, mind, and soul than you've ever realized.

Point number four: you can change your thoughts about money. All you need to do is become aware. You can change your thoughts about money right now, first, by becoming aware of them, and second, by selecting the beliefs you would prefer to have.

You may have beliefs that say, "I want money," but a part of you gets squeamish when you think about having it. This discomfort is only there because of a thought, a belief. Change your thought, change your belief, and you'll have a completely different relationship with money. In order to attract money into your life, you want to change your current thoughts about what's possible and about money itself. This book will show you how.

The fifth point: you can do the impossible financially. You don't know your limits. This is really important for you to grasp. I've talked to people who shrug their shoulders and say, "I can't have what you have. I can't have a new car. I can't have a better job. I can't have a better home. I can't have"—fill in the blank.

They are the ones placing the limits on what's possible for them. We don't know what your limits are; most likely there aren't any at all. We live in a belief-driven universe. Change your beliefs, and you change your universe. You can do the impossible financially, because you are capable of doing anything. There aren't any limits. Moreover, as long as you shoot for the moon, you will go further, stretch more, and get better results than you ever have, so consider that you can do the impossible financially, beginning today.

Number six: whatever abundance image you add emotion to will tend to manifest. Let me explain. An abundance image is the vision you have in your head when it comes to money. If you're worried about money, your abundance image is probably one of scarcity. It's not abundance at all. If you love money, want to have money in your life, and have big dreams for your money to help yourself, your family, your friends, your neighborhood, the world at large, you probably have an abundance image that is very loving and bright and clear.

You have an abundance image of one sort or another. One is probably a negative, darker one, and the other is probably a lighter, brighter one. If you add emotion to either image, it will tend to manifest, and very rapidly. If you have an image of being afraid of money and you add fear to the point where you start to shake and get sweaty palms, you will tend to manifest the very thing that you're worried about.

By the same token—and this is where I want you to put your focus—when you have an abundance image of wealth and prosperity that feels fantastic, and you add the emotion of love, joy, peace, and giddy happiness to it, you will tend to manifest that image instead.

The seventh key point is that you can have money miracles happen in your life when your let go of attachment and need. This is huge. I want you to get it right now:

*you can have virtually anything you want in life as long as you don't need it.* When you need something, you have an energy of desperation around it, and that very energy will go out and attract more desperation.

This is how the law of attraction works. It works with your unconscious beliefs, which you confirm with your energy. If you have an emotion of love, you will tend to attract the thing you love. If you have an emotion of hate, you will tend to attract the thing you hate. If you can have a desire for something without the need for it to come about, then you're in a spirit of letting go. You don't have attachment. You don't have an addiction. You don't have a life-and-death need for it. At that point, your desire is free to be manifested. There's nothing in you that will block it from being attracted into your life.

I can hear what you're thinking right now: "Yes, I want my money miracle, but I've got to pay the rent on Friday," or, "I've got to pay my bills by the end of the month. I need that money. How do I attract money without needing it when I need it?"

I will discuss this question too. I will help you release that desperation, that need, so you'll have a playful desire that says, "I intend to have more money, and I intend to have it before I actually have to pay my bills." You will not attach desperation to it, which means money will come into your life easily and effortlessly.

## MISPERCEPTIONS ABOUT MONEY

Before we go much further, let's talk a little bit about the misperceptions about money. A lot of people think that if they have more money, they're going to be greedy and misuse the wealth.

I once read a delightful old book from 1920, entitled *Fundamentals of Prosperity*, by Roger Babson. He ended his book by asking the president of the Argentine Republic why South America, with all of its natural resources and wonders, was so far behind North America in terms of progress. The president replied, "I have come to this conclusion: South America was settled by the Spanish, who came to South America in search of gold, but North America was settled by the Pilgrim Fathers, who went there in search of God."

Where is your focus, on money or on spirit? On the goals you want or on the spirit that brings them? Money is just a symbol. If you focus on the energy it represents, you will attract it.

Many people are afraid of money because they think they'll become more greedy or they'll misuse the wealth or the power it brings. Where did they get those perceptions? This helps explain where the programming has been coming from in your life. It helps explain why you have not been attracting money so far.

Think about the television shows you watched growing up and the movies that are out there now. Almost all of them characterize wealthy people as greedy, manipulative, and evil. They come across as snobbish and greedy. They are not people you want to be. Many of these misperceptions about greed, power, and wealth have been programmed into your mind by the media. It was entertainment when you watched these shows, but you didn't realize that as you were watching, your subconscious mind was absorbing beliefs. It was concluding, "If I'm wealthy, people won't like me. If I'm wealthy, I'll think greed is good or greed is God. If I'm wealthy, I'll misuse that wealth and power, and I'll ruin myself or others."

These beliefs have been coming from the media, from entertainment, and from other sources. It has nothing to do with your reality or your choices. You can go ahead and attract a great deal of money, knowing that you will use it for good.

This idea helped me the most at a turning point in my life, when I started to make money from my Internet marketing. My books started to come out, and my audio programs started to sell well, so money was coming into my life. I realized that I felt a little uncomfortable with it and that if I didn't get comfortable, I would block the flow and only attract so much money into my life.

I had to stop, reflect, and ask, "What am I going to do with this wealth?" When I realized that the more money I received in my life, the more I was able to help my family, my friends, my community, and even my country, I understood that I could have good reasons for bringing money into my life.

I'll talk about some of these reasons later, but I want you to be aware right now that fears about greed, power, wealth, and what they might do to you are unfounded. They're based on beliefs that you can look at and let go. They don't have to stop you.

Before we go any further, let's find out exactly where your money thermostat is. Let's find out where you are right now with your money mindset. What do you believe about money? What are your thoughts about it? What's going on in your unconscious mind about money right now? You probably don't know; most people don't.

That's why I have a money attractor assessment. This is pivotal and eye-opening. It can open your mind to the inner workings of your own brain. Then we can change what isn't working so that you will be able to attract all the money you want. It'll help you find the little blocks that might need to be straightened out so that you can attract easily and effortlessly.

## MONEY ATTRACTOR ASSESSMENT

Use the 1 to 10 scale to determine your responses to the following questions.

**1. How envious do you feel when you see someone driving an expensive car?**

| 1 | 2 | 3 | 4 | 5 | 6 | 7 | 8 | 9 | 10 |
|---|---|---|---|---|---|---|---|---|---|
| Envious | | | | Nothing | | | | Happy for them | |

**2. How envious do you feel when a coworker gets a raise?**

| 1 | 2 | 3 | 4 | 5 | 6 | 7 | 8 | 9 | 10 |
|---|---|---|---|---|---|---|---|---|---|
| Envious | | | | Nothing | | | | Happy for them | |

**3. How do you feel if you make less money than your parents?**

| 1 | 2 | 3 | 4 | 5 | 6 | 7 | 8 | 9 | 10 |
|---|---|---|---|---|---|---|---|---|---|
| Sad | | | | Nothing | | | | Happy for them | |

**4. How do you feel if you make more money than your parents?**

| 1 | 2 | 3 | 4 | 5 | 6 | 7 | 8 | 9 | 10 |
|---|---|---|---|---|---|---|---|---|---|
| Sad | | | | Nothing | | | | | Proud |

**5. When you come up with an idea, what do you do?**

| 1 | 2 | 3 | 4 | 5 | 6 | 7 | 8 | 9 | 10 |
|---|---|---|---|---|---|---|---|---|---|
| Nothing | | | | Think about it | | | | | Act fast |

**6. Do you give money to worthwhile causes?**

| 1 | 2 | 3 | 4 | 5 | 6 | 7 | 8 | 9 | 10 |
|---|---|---|---|---|---|---|---|---|---|

Not at all                    A little                    I do, regularly


**7. How do you feel about your current home and car?**

| 1 | 2 | 3 | 4 | 5 | 6 | 7 | 8 | 9 | 10 |
|---|---|---|---|---|---|---|---|---|---|

I can do better                Nothing                    I'm happy


**8. What do you do when you want to buy something expensive?**

| 1 | 2 | 3 | 4 | 5 | 6 | 7 | 8 | 9 | 10 |
|---|---|---|---|---|---|---|---|---|---|

Say I can't afford it          Ignore it                    Buy it


**9. Do you feel money is evil?**

| 1 | 2 | 3 | 4 | 5 | 6 | 7 | 8 | 9 | 10 |
|---|---|---|---|---|---|---|---|---|---|

Of course                    Not sure                    Don't know


**10. Do you fear that we will ran out of natural resources such as oil or gas?**

| 1 | 2 | 3 | 4 | 5 | 6 | 7 | 8 | 9 | 10 |
|---|---|---|---|---|---|---|---|---|---|

Of course                                        I'm not sure


**11. What is the meaning you give to money?**

| 1 | 2 | 3 | 4 | 5 | 6 | 7 | 8 | 9 | 10 |
|---|---|---|---|---|---|---|---|---|---|

Necessary evil                None                    Useful tool


**12. What is the definition of money?**

| 1 | 2 | 3 | 4 | 5 | 6 | 7 | 8 | 9 | 10 |
|---|---|---|---|---|---|---|---|---|---|

A tool of greed                Nothing          A medium of exchange

**13. Do you take vacations?**

| 1 | 2 | 3 | 4 | 5 | 6 | 7 | 8 | 9 | 10 |
|---|---|---|---|---|---|---|---|---|----|
| No | | | | Sometimes | | | | | Yes |

**14. Do you read biographies of wealthy people?**

| 1 | 2 | 3 | 4 | 5 | 6 | 7 | 8 | 9 | 10 |
|---|---|---|---|---|---|---|---|---|----|
| No | | | | Sometimes | | | | | Yes |

**15. How do you feel about the richest person in the world?**

| 1 | 2 | 3 | 4 | 5 | 6 | 7 | 8 | 9 | 10 |
|---|---|---|---|---|---|---|---|---|----|
| Envious | | | | Nothing | | | | | Inspired |

**16. If you had all the money you wanted, what would you do?**

| 1 | 2 | 3 | 4 | 5 | 6 | 7 | 8 | 9 | 10 |
|---|---|---|---|---|---|---|---|---|----|
| I don't know | | | | What I'm doing now | | | Travel and enjoy life | | |

**17. Do you feel wealthy right now?**

| 1 | 2 | 3 | 4 | 5 | 6 | 7 | 8 | 9 | 10 |
|---|---|---|---|---|---|---|---|---|----|
| No | | | | Not sure | | | | | Yes |

**18. What do you think of self-employment?**

| 1 | 2 | 3 | 4 | 5 | 6 | 7 | 8 | 9 | 10 |
|---|---|---|---|---|---|---|---|---|----|
| Not good; no security | | | | Not sure | | | | | Great |

**19. What do you think of the current economy?**

| 1 | 2 | 3 | 4 | 5 | 6 | 7 | 8 | 9 | 10 |
|---|---|---|---|---|---|---|---|---|----|
| Desperate | | | | Not sure | | | It doesn't matter | | |

**20. Do you deserve to attract money?**

| 1 | 2 | 3 | 4 | 5 | 6 | 7 | 8 | 9 | 10 |
|---|---|---|---|---|---|---|---|---|----|
| No | | | | | Maybe | | | | Of course |

**21. What did your parents think about money?**

| 1 | 2 | 3 | 4 | 5 | 6 | 7 | 8 | 9 | 10 |
|---|---|---|---|---|---|---|---|---|----|
| Fought over it | | | | Not sure | | | | Not a problem |

**22. Do you invest in your continued learning?**

| 1 | 2 | 3 | 4 | 5 | 6 | 7 | 8 | 9 | 10 |
|---|---|---|---|---|---|---|---|---|----|
| No | | | | Sometimes | | | | | Yes |

**23. Your thoughts about money are generally:**

| 1 | 2 | 3 | 4 | 5 | 6 | 7 | 8 | 9 | 10 |
|---|---|---|---|---|---|---|---|---|----|
| Worried | | | | Varying | | | | | Positive |

**24. Do you have a checking account?**

| 1 | 2 | 3 | 4 | 5 | 6 | 7 | 8 | 9 | 10 |
|---|---|---|---|---|---|---|---|---|----|
| No | | | | | | | | | Yes |

**25. Do you have a savings account?**

| 1 | 2 | 3 | 4 | 5 | 6 | 7 | 8 | 9 | 10 |
|---|---|---|---|---|---|---|---|---|----|
| No | | | | | | | | | Yes |

**26. Do you put money away in case of emergency?**

| 1 | 2 | 3 | 4 | 5 | 6 | 7 | 8 | 9 | 10 |
|---|---|---|---|---|---|---|---|---|----|
| No | | | | | | | | | Yes |

**27. Do you give away 10 percent of your income to people and places that inspire you?**

| 1 | 2 | 3 | 4 | 5 | 6 | 7 | 8 | 9 | 10 |
|---|---|---|---|---|---|---|---|---|----|

No                          Sometimes                          Yes

**28. Do you complain a lot about money and bills?**

| 1 | 2 | 3 | 4 | 5 | 6 | 7 | 8 | 9 | 10 |
|---|---|---|---|---|---|---|---|---|----|

Yes                          Sometimes                          No

**29. How much more money do you think you can have?**

| 1 | 2 | 3 | 4 | 5 | 6 | 7 | 8 | 9 | 10 |
|---|---|---|---|---|---|---|---|---|----|

Not much more              Twice as much          Ten times as much

**30. Do you believe that money corrupts?**

| 1 | 2 | 3 | 4 | 5 | 6 | 7 | 8 | 9 | 10 |
|---|---|---|---|---|---|---|---|---|----|

Yes                          I don't know                          No

**31. Would you rather be honest or rich?**

| 1 | 2 | 3 | 4 | 5 | 6 | 7 | 8 | 9 | 10 |
|---|---|---|---|---|---|---|---|---|----|

Rich over honest          Honest over rich                          Both

**32. Is money hard for you to earn?**

| 1 | 2 | 3 | 4 | 5 | 6 | 7 | 8 | 9 | 10 |
|---|---|---|---|---|---|---|---|---|----|

Yes                          Sometimes                          No

**33. Are you ready to learn the secret to attracting more money?**

| 1 | 2 | 3 | 4 | 5 | 6 | 7 | 8 | 9 | 10 |
|---|---|---|---|---|---|---|---|---|----|

No                          Sometimes                          Yes

Let's look at possible answers. If you scored 33 to 107, you most likely struggle quite a bit with financial issues. Perhaps you've been trying to put opposite poles of the magnet together. In other words, you may need to look at your beliefs and do some emotional, physical, mental, and spiritual reprogramming around your limiting beliefs. Perhaps you feel unworthy to be wealthy or are plagued by old, unsupportive belief systems. Be sure to surround yourself with positive people and reread this book often. Rereading can penetrate your subconscious and change the messages that no longer serve you.

Congratulate yourself for having the courage and insight to purchase this book and keep your commitment to yourself. By doing so, you will likely reach your moneymaking potential faster than you think.

If you scored 108 to 181, you may find yourself feeling stuck in regard to attracting money into your life. Your magnet has lost a great deal of its energy and needs to be replenished. Although you have made some strides, you are not yet fully open to all of the abundance that is here for you. Reading this book and taking actions on its suggestions will energize you and open you up as a vessel to attracting money in your life.

If you scored 182 to 255, you are moving forward towards attracting more money into your life. Keep up the good work and be sure to integrate the new information, practices, and behavior that you learn from this book into your daily regime. Within no time, you will find yourself living a life of abundance financially, emotionally, and creatively.

If you scored 256 to 330, congratulations. You are a money magnet. Whatever you are doing is working. The fact that you purchased this book reflects your commitment to living a life of total abundance. You clearly know how the law of attraction works, and you are drawing what you desire into your life. Continue on your journey. Integrate any material that is new to you, and continue to focus on the specifics of what you wish to manifest. Your magnetism affects the world as a whole and creates positive, wondrous energy for all to enjoy.

This quiz will help you gain clarity on where you stand compared to where you'd like to be. Your answers should be revealing to you. If you have limiting beliefs about money, complain about it, or fear for your security in the future, you will block the flow of money to you. This book will help you dissolve those barriers so you can experience the abundance that you want and deserve.

I suggest that give yourself three months to put the teachings that I am sharing with you into practice. Then do this assessment again, and make note of the terrific progress you've made.

## THINK LIKE AN ENTREPRENEUR

One of the tickets to financial freedom is to think like an entrepreneur. In this book I will teach you how. If you're already an entrepreneur, you already have a business, you're starting a business, or thinking of starting a business, I will show you the finer points of how to market that business.

Don't be turned off by the term *marketing*, because I have a definition for it that you have never heard before, and it has to deal with love and spirit. I will teach you how to use love and spirit in marketing to improve your entrepreneurial results. This is a program that, again, is both practical and spiritual, because at heart I'm what I call a spiritual marketer. I have a foot in the spiritual world and a foot in the marketing world. I combine both to have more power than I could have from either side alone. I think the spiritual and the material are two sides of the same coin, so that when I go forward as a spiritual marketer, I become an entrepreneur of power. In this book I'm going to teach you how to do that as well.

An entrepreneurial mindset for success, combined with a spiritual mindset for success, is the secret to attracting money beyond all comprehension. I've already mentioned the unconscious or subconscious mind and how a lot of the beliefs you have about money are in your unconscious. This is part of the missing secret to attracting money, because most people don't realize that the unconscious is actually the power source. The conscious mind is only the tip of the iceberg. It's where you are thinking your thoughts, but what's really operating your life—including your breathing and heartbeat—is your unconscious. Your beliefs about money and life in general are in your unconscious as well. If you're just trying to make a superficial change—with your thoughts and your conscious mind alone—you're not going to succeed on a permanent basis.

If you want to get real results in attracting money, you have to go to the source. This source isn't a bank, it isn't the Federal Reserve, it isn't a job, it isn't anything more than your own subconscious. Once we get into your subconscious mind and start releasing its beliefs that have been blocking money, you are free to attract money. You may say consciously, "I intend to attract money," but subconsciously, if you have any issue whatsoever with money—you don't know what to do with it, you fear it, or you think that somebody is going to take it from you—you will stop it from coming. Your unconscious beliefs will overrule your conscious intent of having more money.

This process is going to take a little bit of awareness and awakening, but on the other side is financial freedom. I was able to go from being homeless to being a best-selling author and occasional movie star because I worked with my unconscious beliefs. I worked with my sense of deservingness in regard to money, which is based in my unconscious. Once I did that, I opened the pathway to attracting money, and this is going to be true for you too.

Prepare yourself for financial miracles, and I mean that honestly, truthfully, sincerely, with a 100 percent commitment on my part. In this chapter, I've given the seven key points about money, the money assessment quiz, and the idea that if you change your mind and expect financial miracles, you will begin attracting these miracles into your life. All of these combined together are going to shift your mindset as it's never been shifted before. You may have made some attempts to attract money, get a new job, or change your beliefs about abundance, but now is the time for permanent and lasting change, which will never go back and will cause you to attract money as never before.

I want you to play that "What if Up?" game and imagine that this is the greatest moment of your life—that this is the insight, these are the principles, this is the turning point that's going to cause you to attract money unexpectedly and gratefully, in ways that you will be marveling about and joyously sharing with others.

Now is the time for you to attract money. All you have to do is make a commitment to read this book (maybe a couple of times) and expect success.

I am so pleased and grateful to be the one to share this information with you. I look back over my life, and I see how far I've come and what I've had to learn to do this. It's a great honor; it's a great privilege; it's a great moment for me personally. I, the guy who was homeless some fifty years ago, have learned these money attraction secrets, and I get to hold your hand and walk you through them. Deep in my heart, I feel the desire to write this book for you and reveal the secrets. Thank you for this opportunity.

When you're ready to go on, let's continue our journey together in the next chapter.

# TWO
# HOW TO MAKE MONEY IN ANY ECONOMIC CLIMATE

L et me begin by telling you a true and inspiring story about a man who heard that you can make money, that you can attract money, but was a starving musician.

I'm talking about a man who's now my friend, Pat O'Bryan. When Pat came to me back in 2005, he was successful as a musician: he had six or seven CDs out, he was traveling Europe, and he was playing in bars and in clubs in Texas. He was successful in terms of being produced and being paid to perform, but he was starving. He did not have the money to pay his rent. He did not have the money to buy a truck. He was driving around in a beat-up old pickup that in many ways he was proud of, although he never knew if it was going to get him where he needed to go. When he did play for bands and groups, whether it was in this country or in Europe, he was paid $50 for a performance. He was not getting rich.

One time he came up to me, and his face was flushed. He was very angry, and he said, "I need to know how to pay my blankety-blank rent." That moment was a turning point. It's when he decided that what he was doing in his life was not working for him; in many ways it was keeping him stuck. He certainly wanted to attract money. He certainly wanted to have a new truck. He certainly wanted to have more financial experience and wealth. He wanted a new home. He wanted to take care of his wife and kids, but he wasn't able to do it. What he was doing was not working.

So he came to somebody who already knew the secret to attracting money (me) and asked, "How do I do it?" I told him a few things, including that he had to set a new intention. He had to decide that he wanted to attract money easily and effortlessly doing what he loved. That might mean doing something completely different. It meant that he had to open his mind to new possibilities.

So Pat came to one of my seminars called "The Spiritual Marketing Super Summit." He listened to me and the other speakers, and he started to get an entrepreneurial mindset. He decided that he could use his skills as a musician but would create different products—something he'd never thought of before.

Pat started to create subliminal audios. They had powerful affirmations on them, but his were different in that he created original music for these audios. Most people would use Beethoven or some other classical artist that was in the public domain. Pat looked at his own background and thought, "I have skills as a musician, but I'm not making money playing in performances or even with my CDs. I need to create a new product."

Pat came up with subliminal audio recordings that used his own music, and he started selling them. At one of the Spiritual Marketing Super Summits, he was selling so many that he was up all night making more copies, because he was doing it all by hand and selling them the next day.

Pat began to awaken. He saw that he could make money by realizing that he had more talent and experience than he'd ever thought and shifting his mindset. Because he also knew the law of right action, he began to take more action. He came out with forty-five products within the first year. I'm proud of him and dazzled by what he's done and continues to do. He shifted his whole background, his thinking, his belief system so he's still doing music, which he loves, but in a different way. Now it enables him to attract great wealth. Pat used the very principles you're being taught in this book.

When Pat put on his first seminar, he announced it to his list, which he had been developing from the moment when started selling those CDs. After he announced his seminar, he sold it out in six hours. This man has gone on to write books; one became an Amazon best seller. He's got numerous websites up and numerous products out. He and I have made products together, because we've become business partners as well as friends.

All of this came from a man who could not pay his rent and needed to find the secret to attracting money. Part of it was to wake up and realize, "What I've been doing has not been working." That's one of the big insights that anybody has to have in order to start attracting money.

When I was on the streets, I thought I was doing the right thing. I thought that what I was pursuing was going to work out, so I kept on doing the same thing. I think Albert Einstein said it, but I heard it at a Tony Robbins seminar: "If you keep on doing the same thing and getting the same results, it's a form of insanity. What you have to do is change what you're doing." The law of attraction says that what you're doing stems from what you're believing. It isn't the doing that comes first, it's the believing: you have to change the inside of you before you can change the outside.

When Pat looked at his life and decided what he was doing wasn't working, he had to look at his own beliefs and say, "My belief system isn't getting me the results I want. What belief system *will* get me the results I want?" He turned to me and began to model himself on what I was doing and saying. He read my books and listened to my audios, and then of course he took action.

This is how you make money in any economic climate. You shift from the outer to the inner. It doesn't matter what the economic climate is; your mental climate is what matters.

## PRINCIPLES FOR A NEW MINDSET

Let me talk about some of the principles you have to incorporate in order to take on this new mindset.

### 1. BELIEVE IN YOURSELF

The first one is, you have to believe in yourself. You have to believe in the power of your own heart and mind to change your financial situation. This first principle is basically saying, "Believe in you." You may not believe in you right now, you may have not decided to trust yourself up until this moment, but I'm here to encourage you. I'm here to say, "If Pat can make the change, and I can make the change, and hundreds and thousands of other people can make the change, then you can do it too." It begins by believing in your own heart, in your own mind. Believing in you. Believing in your desires. Believing in the good within you to take care of you.

## 2. THE UNIVERSE LOVES YOU

The second principle is to believe in a kind and harmonious universe that supports you financially. Basically, you believe that the universe loves you. Most people who are struggling, including myself nearly fifty years ago, thought it was me against the universe. I did not believe that the universe was on my side. I did not believe that the universe loved me. I felt that it was me against the planet and that I was totally alone. Pat felt the same way. He felt it was him against the world: he and his guitar could lick the world. That's an ego trip; it's self-sabotage. That doesn't work.

The universe actually loves you; it is supporting you right now by keeping you alive. The universe will support your financial desires if you believe it will. The universe will support anything you believe. It's up to you to be in alignment with the universe. The universe is saying yes to you right now. If you've been thinking that money is bad, the universe is basically saying, "OK, if that's what you believe, I will support you in your decision." The universe comes from a place of love and support. When you align your unconscious mind with it, you're able to attract money. So the second principle is to know that you are loved.

### 3. BELIEVE IN A HIGHER SOURCE

The third principle is to believe in a benevolent higher source that supports your financial desires. This is an extension of what I just talked about, but it's a little more refined. With this third principle, you understand that you can ask for help and get it. This higher source, this greater power, whatever you want to call this being of which we're all a part, is actually here to give you what you want. It supports your money desires and your financial interest, but you have to ask for help from it.

This, I confess, was one of the big secrets to turning my life around. When I began to look for and ask for help from something bigger than me, I started to receive it, and I started to attract money. I'll talk about this a little more detail later, when I give you some of the processes for cleaning up your limiting beliefs about money. But for now, step three says, believe that there is a higher power that supports your financial desires. It's actually there to answer your requests.

### 4. GIVE UP VICTIMHOOD

The fourth principle is to give up reacting as a victim to outer financial challenges. Unfortunately, almost everybody is born into the stage of feeling like a victim, and almost everybody goes to their death feeling like a victim, but you want to awaken from that.

In this fourth step, you give up reacting to outer financial challenges as a victim, meaning that you start to take your power back. You start to realize that you and your unconscious/subconscious mind are the source of the greatest power within you. You don't have to pay attention to the economic climate. You don't have to react to the financial challenges reported in the media, because the outer has nothing to do with your inner. Change your inner, and you create a different outer circumstance. That's step four: give up reacting.

## 5. FORGIVE

Number five is a big one: forgive yourself and others for financial wrongdoings. This is both a spiritual and a psychological insight. When you forgive yourself and everybody else involved with anything that you thought was wrong in your career, you free the energy that's been stuck within you.

This point is earthshaking. Say you hold a grudge against somebody who did something at work—maybe it was a boss, a supervisor, a coworker; maybe it was some sort of injustice. It may have happened last week or last decade, but you are still thinking about it. Thinking about it is eating up your energy. That energy is being kept alive within you, but it's not being used to create more money. When you have something within you that you've not released and you've not forgiven somebody for it, you have a memory alive within you that is using up your energy and your mental system. When you release your grudges, you release that energy to allow something new and greater to come in.

The money that you've been wanting will come to you when you release this bound up energy within you. That bound up energy is in a place of a lack of forgiveness. You have to look at your own life and say, "I did the best I can. I forgive myself for everything that I've ever done, that I ever thought was incorrect, and I forgive everybody else around me."

I think forgiving is one of the greatest steps you can take to cleanse yourself of blocks to attracting money. Later I will guide you through some processes that will help you forgive. But for now understand this fifth insight: when you forgive yourself and others for financial wrong-doings, you open yourself to attracting more money.

## 6. BE GRATEFUL

Number six, be grateful for everything that comes your way. Gratitude may be single-handedly the most powerful money magnet that I can think of. I first heard about the power of gratitude when I was in poverty in Houston. I heard about it numerous times at churches that I went to. I read about it in magazines and books like Catherine Ponder's *The Dynamic Laws of Prosperity*. I kept thinking, "Why do they keep talking about gratitude?" Because when you feel grateful, you become a magnet for more experiences to be grateful for. In my skeptical mind, I thought, "Yeah. I'll be grateful when I have money. I'll be grateful when I have a job. I'll be grateful when I have that relationship. I'll be grateful when I have the house. I'll be grateful when"—fill in the blank. But I've learned that's not how it works. You actually want to be grateful now. As you are, you start to attract more of what you wanted in the first place. You don't wait to begin the process of gratitude; you begin it now.

When I first heard about this principle decades ago, I was skeptical. I remember picking up a pencil, holding it, and saying, "OK, I can be grateful for a pencil." But I was not really being grateful; I was being a smart aleck about it. Then I looked at the pencil and I thought, "OK, with this piece of lead I could write a suicide note, or a grocery list, or a to-do list, or a love letter, or a letter to the editor, or the great American novel." As I looked at it, I started to think, "Gosh, the pencil is actually pretty amazing. What a miraculous tool. It's actually a twig. It's a piece of wood with lead in it, but I can use it to write anything that my mind conjures up." I started to move into this place of truly feeling amazed and grateful for the pencil.

Then I looked at the other side, which had an eraser. I thought, "What is this piece of rubber? Whoever thought of that? Well, this piece of rubber can help me erase the suicide note, the love letter, the things I've already bought on my shopping list, even the parts of the great American novel I don't like."

I looked at the pencil and thought, "This is a work of genius. It is a breathtaking masterpiece. I can write anything I want on one side, and if I screw up, there's an eraser on the other side."

I moved into a place of gratitude. By feeling grateful for that pencil, I opened my heart to see new opportunities for ways of making and attracting money and to see that there were things to be grateful for all around me. That was the window that opened up and changed my life when I was in poverty. It all began by being grateful for a pencil. So, again, the sixth insight is that being grateful for all that comes your way will help you attract more money.

## 7. TAKE ACTION

The seventh one is, take action. I'm the guy in the movie *The Secret* who says, "The universe loves speed." I'm also the guy who says, "Money loves speed." This has almost become my motto: when I get an idea, I act on it, and I act quickly. When you get an idea, I encourage you to act on it and act right now.

There are reasons for acting right away. I'll give you a quick one: when you receive a moneymaking idea, a way to attract a lot of money right now, it comes with a great deal of energy—a kind of orgasmic rush. You feel excited;

you feel energized. You can use that energy to turn that idea into reality.

When I get an idea for a book, more often than not I will stop everything and start writing it. I'm honoring the idea; I think ideas are gifts from the universe, which come to me unannounced and unbidden for. I give my thanks for the idea and honor it by taking action as quickly as possible. When I take that action, I'm using the energy that came with the idea to accomplish it faster.

Here's another reason for acting quickly: have you, after having an idea for a product or service, ever walked into a store and saw it on the shelf? Somebody else brought it into being. This happens all the time. I believe that the universe is giving the same idea to a half a dozen or more people at any one point. When you get an idea for a product, a service, a book, or whatever it happens to be, it's not just coming to you; it's coming to several people at the same time. If you don't act on it, one or more of those people are going to act on it. One day, six months or six years from now, you'll walk into a store and you'll see your idea being sold. So taking action is the seventh principle.

It's very important that as soon as you have a chance, you take time to play with these seven principles: read them and write them down for yourself. It's one thing to just read them, but you want to make them a part of your living, breathing soul.

## FIVE STEPS FOR ATTRACTING MONEY

Maybe at this point you're wondering how can you best affect the outer world, to turn it into a safer, heartier, more abundant place. You may be wondering how you can get to the place where you're attracting money in any economic climate. I have a five step formula to help you do that. They have been proved to work over and over again. People have used them to attract cars, relationships, cash, health—anything that you can imagine. Here are the five steps:

### 1. KNOW WHAT YOU *DON'T* WANT

Although this might seem very obvious, many people still play the victim. They talk about what they don't want but they stay there; they don't go past it.

I think it's insightful to know what you don't want. Take an inventory of your complaints. If you don't want the job you have, the amount of money you have, or the bills or debts that you have—whatever it happens to be— make a list of these things. Make a list: "These are the things I *don't* want when it comes to money." Vocalize them. Take a mental inventory of them, write them all down, and then purge them from your brain. That's the first step.

## 2. INTEND WHAT YOU PREFER

Why did we do that? It's healing and cathartic to get these things out on paper. In addition, you use this step to springboard into step two: *intend what you prefer.* Ask yourself, "What do you want? How much money do you want? What kind of job do you want? What kind of position? What kind of business? What kind of sales? What kind of entrepreneurial results?"

Look at everything you wrote down in step one: all your complaints, all the things you said you didn't want. Take them and turn them around 180 degrees. If you said "I don't want this debt," you could turn that complaint into an intention: "I have more than enough money to pay off all of my bills," or, "I have paid all of my bills, and I'm now financially free," or even, "I have more than enough money to pay whatever bill comes before it even arrives."

You state your intention using a phraseology that makes the most sense to you. It has to feel good to you; it has to be believable to you.

You want to go through this process for a couple of reasons. First of all, when you state an intention, your body and mind go in the direction of that intention. You realign your whole energy system. Your unconscious mind, your conscious mind, and your body all go in the direction of that intention. It's very powerful.

Another reason for doing this process has a spiritual as well as a psychological aspect: when you state your intention, you send out a message to the universe. It then rearranges you and everybody else, much like chess pieces on a board, to fulfill your intention. This is where magic and miracles come into play. You might end up running into somebody that can fulfill your desire. Or you suddenly open up a magazine and see an ad that answers your intention. It all happens with great synchronicity because you stated a clear intention.

Step one, then, is to state your complaints. Step two is to change your complaints into intentions.

## 3. GET CLEAR

Step three is, *get clear.* That is, get clear of your unconscious limiting beliefs you've had about money. If you say, "I want to attract money" while unconsciously thinking money is bad, you're going to veto your conscious desire, and you won't attract the money.

In this step, you do whatever it takes. Later I'll walk you through some belief cleansing and clearing processes. Here you're getting rid of the internal blocks that have been stopping you from having the money you want. When you get clear of that inner interference, money just comes in. There's nothing blocking it anymore. Now you're free to attract it.

## 4. NEVILLIZE YOUR GOAL

Step four is, *Nevillize your goal*. *Nevillize* is a word I've coined after the inspirational author Neville Goddard (1905–72), whom I greatly love. His books and recordings are still available, and I encourage you to read and listen to them. Neville believed that if you can imagine the end result of what you want as if it's already come to pass, you will actually turn it into concrete reality.

Neville was a mystic who was very much ahead of his time, but I have found his system to be valid. Although visualization and mental imagery are great, if you want to attract money into your life at warp speed, if you really want to press down on the accelerator, you have to Nevillize your goal. This means to imagine that you've already achieved it, and to do it with great feeling.

When you Nevillize your goal, you go the end result of your intention. If you said, "I now have $5,000 of unexpected income that showed up on Friday," *now* refers to events that have already taken place. You take a deep breath, close your eyes, and imagine what it feels like to have that $5,000 in unexpected income *now*, in your hands, right this moment. I could look at my checking account and see it there. Or if you say that you want a particular job, or you want to break a sales record, or you want have any number of financial rewards coming in any number of ways, what does that feel like in your experience now? One way to imagine this is to pretend it's the end of the day when you've attained your goal. In your journal, you write, "Today I've achieved financial independence. It happened unexpectedly, it happened joyously, and this is how I feel." You write this down in the past tense, focusing on the end result and the good feelings that come from it.

When you Nevillize your goal, you go beyond affirmations and visualizations. Neville said that you enter a fourth dimension with this thought form. It doesn't matter that it hasn't come to pass yet. In your mind, you imagine that you have the end result. When you do that with feeling, that Nevillized goal goes into the fourth dimension and begins to take root. Before you know it, you attract money in this dimension, in the real world that you and I know. That's step four: Nevillize your goal.

## 5. TAKE INSPIRED ACTION

The fifth and final step is, *let go while taking inspired action*. To let go while taking inspired action means to be detached from your desire. Again, if you want something too much, you're actually going to push it away, because that feeling of desperation is going to cause you to trip yourself up. You will sabotage yourself. You can't *need* your result. When you do, you believe you are not complete without it, and this will become a self-fulfilling prophecy. You have to let go of your need; you have to let go of your attachment; you have to let go of any addiction to the end result. You have to be able to say, "It would be wonderful if I had this money in my life, but I won't die without it." You have to come from a place of neutrality, a place of peace.

Even though you come from a place of peace, you don't sit and do nothing. That's why the fifth step is to let go while taking inspired action. Because you've taken all of these steps in this process, you're going to be nudged from within to do something; it might be to buy a book or a program, open a business, answer an ad, or get a loan. When you feel that inspired nudge to do something, you're part of the process of attracting more money. As I said, you have to take action: the universe likes speed; money likes speed. Let go of your addiction to having your result work out the way you expect it to. Let go of any demand for it to happen in a certain way; at the same time, take inspired action.

To recap, these are the five steps in the process of attracting money:

1. Know what you *don't* want.
2. Declare your intentions. Turn your complaints into statements of objectives.
3. Get clear of your limiting and negative beliefs.
4. Nevillize your goal: imagine that your desire has already come to pass. What does that feel like? Find a way to anchor it in your mind, if only for a moment.

5. Let go of your need for things to work out a certain way while taking inspired action, so that you are participating in the process of cocreating and attracting money.

## PROTECT YOURSELF FROM NEGATIVE MESSAGES

From time to time, you're going to hear people gossiping around the water cooler, you're going to hear the news, you're going to hear something over the media, and you're going to start to worry. How do you protect yourself? How can you armor yourself against the negative messages that surround money?

I have five suggestions. The first is to ignore water cooler gossip. At one point decades ago, I worked for a big oil company. I learned where the support was and where the negativity was, and I stayed away from the negativity. Very often it happens around the coffee bar, the water cooler, or the smoking areas. You can choose to walk away and go where there is support. You can choose to tune out the gossip.

You also have a choice when it comes to the media. Many positive programs and news shows are out there, as well as a great deal of negative programming. I say turn off the negative news. I don't pay attention to the media. I don't read the newspaper. I don't watch the news.

I once interviewed the late Bill Bartmann, a billionaire who was once homeless. He told me that he looked at the news for three minutes or so, just to get a sense of the big stories, but he didn't buy into the news. I don't even think you need to listen to the three minutes, but if you want to hear the main stories, maybe tune in for a few minutes and move on.

My belief is that the media have been structured to find the most negative news out there. Because they are a highly refined persuasion tool, they know how to feed negativity right into your brain. Unless you create a force field around your mind, it's very difficult to watch the media with any neutrality. So my second step is to say, "Turn it off."

The third step is to read positive material. Find positive magazines, positive articles, positive websites, and positive books, and feed your mind something healthy.

The fourth thing is to listen to positive material, such as audio programs. Feed your mind with positive material through your ears.

The fifth step—and this is incredibly powerful—is to get support. You can, for example, create a Master Mind. A Master Mind is when you get five or six people (usually not more than that, usually not less than three) who are supporting one another in going for their dreams. You can create a Master Mind around this book. You can get five or six people who take turns talking about their financial goals. You all supply ideas, information, and resources to help one another attract more money. Having a Master Mind, a group of friends to support you, is one way to protect yourself from media messages about the economic climate, which at this point we know doesn't even matter.

Another thing you can do is get coaching. With coaching, you have somebody outside of your mental limitations helping you stretch, helping you see your possibilities as well as your belief limitations so that you can change them.

Another way of getting support is to have a friend, somebody like a miniature Master Mind, with whom you can share what you're trying to do, and you can provide the same support system for them as well.

To recap, there are at least five things that you can do to repel negative messages:

1. Ignore water cooler gossip.
2. Turn off the media.
3. Read positive written material.
4. Listen to positive material.
5. Get support through a Master Mind, coaching, friends or any number of other ways.

## KARMIC MARKETING

You're probably wondering why it seems to take so long to attract what you want. How can you attract money faster and more easily? I don't blame you for asking those questions; I've asked them in the past. I think that the only thing that slows anybody down from attracting money is their own mindset, their own belief system. Again we're going to go into detail to see which of your beliefs might be snags in the process. As you release these beliefs, as you get clear, you'll streamline the process of attracting wealth, money, or anything else into your life. Once you get rid of the blocks within you, you are free to bring what you want to you.

Nevertheless, there are some tricks we can use. One is what I call *karmic marketing*. I've made that expression up. It really has to do with giving. I have found that when you give what you want to attract, you will attract more of it. Once I wrote a little book called *The Greatest Money Making Secret in History*. I still love that little book, mostly because of the title, but it refers to one thing: giving. If you want to circulate money into your life, you begin by giving it away.

Decades ago, when first heard this idea, I thought, "How can I give money? I don't have any money to give. I have nothing." When I was ruthlessly honest, I realized I was lying to myself. Even when I had $1 in my pocket, that was a piece of money I could give away. I could give away 10 percent of it; I could give away a dime. But my mentality was one of scarcity, so I thought, "I can't give that dollar away, because I need that dollar."

Can you see the beliefs at work? Can you see programming at work? This is the very mindset that prevents money from being attracted into your life. You have to let it go. Money has to be circulated. I learned that when I started to give away money. When I did this every time I received spiritual or inspirational nourishment, I found that the money would tend to come back to me fairly quickly. It came back to me even faster once I cleaned up my beliefs and got away from the limitations in my mind. The more money I would give away, the more I would receive.

I've talked to other wealthy people who have been doing their best to give away money, and they can't seem to do it. After Percy Ross became a multimillionaire, he dedicated the rest of his life to giving away his money. When he died, his wealth was worth about ten times more than when he started to give it away. In short, he couldn't give it away. As he tried to, more money kept coming to him.

I've experimented with karmic marketing over the course of my life. Once when I was working for the oil company in Houston, I went to lunch. After years of doing the same old thing, I went into a neighborhood I'd never been to before and came across an Italian deli. I was new to Texas. I was born and raised in Ohio with an Italian family, so having authentic Italian food was a regular thing that I could no longer get. When I saw the Italian deli, I immediately pulled in, went inside, and found a wonderful little man from Italy who was selling the most authentic Italian food I'd had since I left the Buckeye State.

I got a sandwich, went back to my office, and ate it. I had tears in my eyes, because I thought, "This reminds me of home. This reminds me of the foods that I've been longing for and missed."

I called up the fellow at the Italian deli and said, "I was just in your deli, and I just ordered a sandwich."

"Yeah," he said. He was defensive, because he thought I was going to complain.

"I want you to know that this was the best sandwich I've eaten in probably fifteen years. It was absolutely awesome."

He thanked me. I got off the phone and thought, "He doesn't really get it. He doesn't know just how much he's impacted me."

I closed my office door and spent that afternoon rewriting the deli menu. I made it far more appetizing with hypnotic writing and made it far more graphically appealing with some visuals. I laid it out using the company equipment at my disposal. When I was done, I looked at the menu and thought, "This is really good." I printed off a thousand copies and posted that menu on every bulletin board in the two buildings in the area where I was working.

The next day, I went over to have another meal at the deli. The man's parking lot was full. There was a line coming out the door. He saw me and came running out with tears in his eyes to say, "I can't believe you've done this."

"Done what?"

"You wrote this menu; apparently you put it up at the oil company, because all these people are coming over to eat."

"That's nothing," I said and showed him the thousand copies that I had printed up. I gave them to him and said, "This is all for you."

I did this out of a sense of gratitude, because I wanted to give. I gave without expecting anything in return, but I didn't have to pay for a meal for the next year and a half: every time I went there, the man gave me whatever I wanted.

But the story gets even better. A few years later, my wife at that time and I wanted to move. I was going to leave the oil company, finances were very tight, and our credit wasn't so great. I wanted to find a home to move into, but I couldn't do it with poor credit. My Italian deli friend told me that his home, which he had built for himself and in which his whole family had been raised, had been empty for a year. He wanted to sell it, but he didn't want it to go to just anybody. He sold it to me. He financed it, making it easy for us to get it. My wife and I lived in it for twelve years; when we separated, she stayed in it until she passed away. This all came from giving.

You can give anything that you want to receive. Let me give an example of karmic marketing on a different level. At one point I heard about a little boy who had had a stroke six weeks after birth. His name is Kirk. I never met Kirk, and I still haven't, nor have I met his mother. But I heard the story from a mutual friend, who said that after the stroke, Kirk was paralyzed. He needed a particular machine to help him retrain his body and mind so he could move his limbs.

When I saw pictures of little Kirk, he seemed to be the happiest little guy on the planet. I thought, "Somebody needs to do something." I heard that the machine cost $15,000. I took a deep breath. I don't know what $15,000 means to you, but $15,000 means a lot to me, any way you look at it. Nevertheless, I wrote a check for $15,000 and sent it to Kirk's mom.

I expected little Kirk to get better. I hoped they would send me photos of him and that I could shake his little hand, but I gave $15,000 for that machine with no expectation of return.

Later the same day, I received $35,000 in unexpected income, which was much more than I had given for Kirk's exercise machine. This money came out of the blue. I was absolutely delighted by it, but I did not expect it. It truly was a surprise to me.

This is how you attract money when you start giving away, when you start implementing the principle of karmic marketing. If you want to speed up the process of attracting money, you have to give. Give money, give whatever you can, to wherever you receive spiritual and inspirational nourishment. It doesn't have to be money; it can be skills. When I wrote the menu for the Italian deli, I was using skills I had and equipment I had access to at that point.

When I wrote that check for $15,000, I probably felt better about it than about most of the checks I've ever written in my life. Part of me was beaming and feeling so sunshiny that something inside opened up. I think that's what goes on when you start giving: something inside you opens up to a degree that you've never experienced before. That opening allows money to flow back to you.

I'm doing many more things with marketing. For example, I'm starting a movement to end foreclosures and homelessness in the United States. It's called Operation Yes! *Yes* stands for *your economic salvation*.

In short, if you really want to speed up the process of attracting more money, give. Give money, give service, give skills, give time, give energy, but give. The more you give, the more you open yourself to receiving. It's a wonderful way to make a difference in your own life, in your community's life, and even in the world. This is one of the greatest tips that I can share with you at this point.

Again, if you want to attract money, you definitely have to give money. If you don't, it's because you have a mindset based in fear. You have a block within you that says, "If I give my money, I won't get any more." That's scarcity thinking. That's victimhood thinking. That is a fear mindset, and it will actually block money from coming to you.

I was in the same place. I was right where you were. I believed that if I gave money, I wouldn't get any more. It took me forever to realize what I hope you realize right now: when you give money, you will begin to attract money.

I'm not talking about emptying your pocketbook or savings account. I am telling you that you need to give some money, generally 10 percent, to wherever you receive inspirational or spiritual nourishment. That's up to you. If you're not giving away money right now, it's a sign of a block. It's why you're not attracting money: there's a belief and a fear that there won't be any more. If you look at that fear closely, it's a great joke, because money always circulates.

You always get more money. If you actually emptied your pocketbook or your wallet right now and gave it to a homeless person right this moment, you would know that you're going to attract some money some way, either today or tomorrow or the next day. It's the nature of the universe to fill a vacuum. But if you hold on to this money, you're maintaining a belief that there isn't enough and that you're not going to get any more and maybe don't even deserve any more.

Giving away money is essential to attracting money, and I encourage you to do it today. Think about where have you have been inspired, spiritually fed, or encouraged. Give 10 percent of what you're carrying right now to that person, place, or thing. Do it now. It's taking that first step. Do it.

## DISCOVER YOUR LIFE MISSION

To round off this chapter, I want to invite you to go through a process to discover your life mission. This is fun; I do it from time to time just to find out what my next steps are. In his book *Ask and You Shall Receive*, Pierre Morency says you must ask for what you want. Asking gives you focus and directs the energy of the universe to manifest it with you.

The cover of Morency's book asks, "What did you ask for when you got up this morning?" I love the question, and I'm now asking it every morning when I awaken. It's my breakfast.

Another question in the book can help you find your passion. Morency asks, "What would you do if you possessed all the money in the world? What would you do if you could make money appear by simply snapping your fingers? What would you do once you owned twelve houses, made fourteen exotic trips, and bought twenty-eight luxury cars?"

How would you answer this question? Your answer is a major clue to your calling, your life purpose, your passion. Don't take this as a light exercise; don't be flippant about it. I think there's great depth to it. Pause and play with the possibility that you've just won the lottery, received an inheritance, or by reading this book attracted enough money to be independently wealthy.

Now that you have all the money you've ever dreamed of, what are you going to do? Knowing the answer will help you uncover your life purpose, and when you follow your life purpose, you tend to attract money easily, quickly, and effortlessly.

# THREE
# NINE SECRETS FOR ATTRACTING MONEY

In this chapter, I'm going to talk about the nine secrets to attracting money. Because I'm an entrepreneur, results-oriented man, I need to get results. All of these nine secrets will help you attract money. They're, in fact, guaranteed to help you attract money.

## JOE'S NINE SECRETS TO ATTRACTING MONEY
1. Give money away.
2. Get clear.
3. Take action.
4. Support a cause.

5. Get support.
6. Be grateful.
7. Do what you love.
8. Elevate your thinking.
9. Problems create opportunities.

## GIVE MONEY AWAY

Let's jump right in, look at secret number one: *give money away*. Let me remind you that if you're resistant to giving money away, it's a sign that you have a block about money. You have a feeling or a fear that there's not enough to go around, that there is a scarcity, or that you personally, out of the 7.5 billion people on the planet, aren't going to receive more money if you give it away. You need to look at that.

## GET CLEAR

Secret number two is to *get clear.* I've talked about this already, but now I want to describe a belief-cleansing process for money.

You take a belief about money, and you begin to find the positive benefit for it; then you extend this in turn to find a positive benefit for the benefit. I will walk you through this so it makes more sense.

What is a belief that you have about money? It could be that money's bad for you. It could be that there isn't enough money to go around. It could be that money is evil. It could be that money is going to contaminate you. It could be that money is going to cause the IRS to come after you. There's probably a belief that surfaced right away as you read this. If there wasn't, just pick one of the ones I've just mentioned so you can go through this exercise. You can do it mentally or in writing.

You have a belief, say, "Money is bad for me." Then you ask, "What's the positive benefit for the belief that money is bad for you?" It could be that the belief protects you from being hurt. In other words, it has a positive benefit. "Believing that money is bad for me protects me from being hurt," so you would write that down.

Then you'd say, "What's the positive benefit from that benefit?" Say you answer, "That belief protects me from being hurt." What's the positive benefit for that belief? It might be that you get to stay safe. Staying safe is the benefit in believing that the belief that money is bad for me is protecting you from being hurt.

Then ask, "What's the positive benefit from staying safe?" It could be that you're not judged, or you feel you are normal. It could be that by staying safe, you feel you are not going to be judged by other people. That's the benefit from the previous benefit.

When you write all of this out, it will make far more sense. If you follow along and let it be an easily unfolding process, you'll reach a surprising conclusion. You'll end up looking at your original belief, "Money is bad for me," with your ending positive benefit: "Believing money is bad for me keeps me from being judged. It keeps me feeling safe."

If you write this out, you'll end up with a statement much like this: "The belief that money is bad for me causes me to feel safe and not judged."

Now this becomes very interesting, because when you realize that you find several layers of benefits to a belief that actually doesn't serve you, you end up with this insight: "That belief is actually toxic to me." The belief "Money is bad for me," although it has positive benefits, ends up being a statement that does not serve you.

In this particular case, "Money is bad for me" is a belief that is keeping you safe, but is it? Money is a means of exchange; in itself, it's just energy. There's no meaning to it. But if you don't have money, you can't pay your bills. You can't pay for your car. You can't pay for your utilities. You can't pay for your home. You can't pay for the luxuries or even the needs of life. Is the belief "Money is bad for me" keeping you safe? Is that actually a positive belief that serves you?

When you look at it in depth, you realize that the belief "Money is bad for me" is actually hurting you; it's limiting you. When you see this belief from this deep perspective, you start to realize that it doesn't serve you. When you understand that this belief doesn't serve you, it starts to break away from your system.

Beliefs are software for the mind. They are part of the programming that keeps you getting the results you are getting right now. When you think, "Money is bad for me," do you really believe you're going to attract money? No, you're going to push it away. You're going to find reasons not to have it. You may consciously say, "I want money," but if you have the belief "Money is bad for me," you will block it. You will find ways not to bring it into your life. You will do anything possible, and you'll do it unconsciously to prevent money from being attracted in your world.

This belief cleansing process shines a deep, penetrating light on a belief. You can do this for any belief.

## BELIEF CLEANSING PROCESS

Try this practice. You can write your answers in this book if you like.

My original belief is:

_____

_____

_____

_____

_____

The benefit I get from asserting this belief is:

_____

_____

_____

_____

_____

The consequent belief I have is:

_____

_____

_____

_____

_____

The benefit I get from asserting this belief is:

_____

_____

_____

_____

_____

The realization I have is:

_____

_____

_____

_____

_____

When you dissect these beliefs, you realize that they may not be serving you, and you can let them go. You're playing detective here. You are diagramming a belief to find out its perceived benefits. Then you're stating the belief with the benefits that you've been tying to it and ask, is this serving me? When you find out it has not been serving you, you are free to let it go; surprisingly, it often starts to leave all by itself. Again, this is another way to get clear of limiting beliefs. It's secret number two in the nine steps to attracting money. Getting clear is another step in attracting the wealth you want.

## TAKE ACTION

Secret number three is to *take action*. I've spent quite a bit of time talking about action, but I want to remind you that if you have an idea right now to do something, you should be taking action on it. Your part in the cocreation process to attract more money is to act on the ideas that are coming to you. If you're not acting on them, it means you're afraid. You are afraid of failure, or you are afraid of success.

Get clear of these beliefs, because when you can take inspired action, you can bring in more money without interference, delay, or self-sabotage. As I've already said, the universe likes speed. Money likes speed.

## SUPPORT A CAUSE

Number four is to *support a cause.* People in general don't feel they deserve good things in their lives. A long time ago, I discovered this psychological insight: one way around this belief is to trick yourself into believing you deserve money by supporting a cause. When you start to think outside of yourself, and you start to think about people other than yourself, you expand your ability to receive.

As I've mentioned, I created Operation Yes! to help end foreclosures and homelessness in this country. On one level, this goal sounds bizarre and preposterous. How can anybody do that? It all begins with a thought. (Below I'll talk about how to elevate your thinking.)

I started Operation Yes! partly to get over my traumatic experience as a homeless person, and partly because I had already lived through it, and I knew that people could get out of these situations with support, skills, training, and help. By starting Operation Yes!, I was doing something bigger than my own ego.

That's the secret. It doesn't have to be a cause that you start yourself, but when you support a cause, you start to get out of your own mental limitations. When you act only for yourself, when you want money only for yourself, your ego kicks in. Your ego limitations slam down on you, closing off your ability to attract money. You'll only allow so much in.

When you support a cause, you're doing something for people other than yourself. This expands your mind, your heart, and your ability to receive.

Support a cause. It's a great way to expand your ability to receive money. Find or create one you can believe in.

## GET SUPPORT

Secret number five is to *get support*. As I've already indicated, this could mean getting coaching. It could mean creating a Master Mind group. It could mean just having a friend that you can share your ideas with. In any case, I think getting support is one of the greatest million-dollar secrets for attracting money.

Trying to be a Lone Ranger in life and doing everything by yourself is a surefire means of self-sabotage. When I was going through poverty in Houston, for the longest time I was trying to do it by myself; I was a Lone Ranger. I went to seminars, where I heard that if you're trying to do everything by yourself, you're on an ego trip. If you really want to have success, help other people and let other people help you. Getting support is a wonderful way to attain results.

I don't mean get financial support. I'm not talking about getting a loan (though that might be a useful action step at some point). I'm talking about having the emotional and psychological support that comes from having somebody who believes in you. Somebody who says, "You can do it." Somebody who says, "Go ahead and reach for the moon, for the stars, for whatever you want." Somebody who is supporting you in your goals to be financially free. That's a big secret, secret number five.

## BE GRATEFUL

Secret number six is *being grateful*. I've already mentioned beginning my process of gratitude by picking up a pencil—a inexpensive, yellow, number two pencil—and starting to feel grateful for it. You don't have to use a pencil, you don't have to do anything in particular, but look around right now and find something, anything, for which you are genuinely grateful. It could be for the sky; it could be for your arms, your watch, your clothes, your life, your relationship, or your pet. Find anything for which you genuinely, in this moment, feel grateful.

Real magic kicks in here. This is a very spiritual as well as psychological principle: when you feel grateful for what's in this moment, you start to attract more things to be grateful for.

I live in a luxury estate, and I have a hot tub outside, under the Texas stars. I get in it almost every night. When I'm in it, I look up at the stars and say, "Thank you. Thank you for my life. Thank you for everything that happened this day. Thank you for the results. Thank you for the benefits"—whatever they happen to be. I focus on gratitude. As I feel this gratitude, my heart opens, my eyes water up, and sometimes I even cry. It's a wonderful place to be.

Because I feel grateful every night and as many times as possible during the day, I attract more money, more experiences, more awards, more movies, more TV shows, more books, more—fill in the blank. These things rush into my life with joyous surprise; I no longer have to make them happen.

A wonderful thing occurs when you learn the secret to attracting money: you move into a place of gratitude. You're grateful in this moment, and all the moments after it get better and better; you don't have to do much more than being grateful in the moment.

Being grateful is something you can do right now. Take a breath and say, "I am grateful for this book," or—fill in the blank. Find something you feel grateful for, and move into that energy right now.

## DO WHAT YOU LOVE

Secret seven: *do what you love*. This point should not come as any surprise, because people have talked about doing what you love for the longest time. Joseph Campbell said, "Follow your bliss." Author Marsha Sinetar said, "Do what you love, and the money will follow."

I rephrase this principle. Interviewers have often asked, "Joe, to what do you owe your secret to success? How'd you go from homeless to multimillionaire? How'd you go from there to here?" I say, "Basically, I followed my enthusiasms." I follow my heart. I follow my passion. I follow the things that I've been excited about, curious about, enthused about.

When I was researching my book on P.T. Barnum, *There's a Customer Born Every Minute*, I was fascinated by this man. Contrary to popular belief, he never said, "There's a sucker born every minute." It's an urban myth. Although he was a genius at marketing, he was actually very spiritual. His neighbors called him Reverend Barnum, because he was so spiritual and so much into understanding life. He really knew about the power of letting go. The epitaph on his little concrete tombstone in Bridgeport, Connecticut, says, "Not my will, but thine be done."

I wrote my book on Barnum because of my personal fascination with him. I did not know that it would cause me to be on PBS or that it would be one of my first best sellers. I was simply doing what I loved. I have found over and over again that when you follow your heart (while using these other secrets), you go in the direction of attracting money. When you follow your heart, you seem to be moving into alignment with the universe. The universe seems to reward you with things like money. Secret number seven is to do what you love.

## ELEVATE YOUR THINKING

Secret number eight is to *elevate your thinking*. As Einstein said, "You cannot solve the problems you have with the same mentality that created them."

How do you change your mentality? How do you elevate your thinking? There are four stages of awakening. The first is *victimhood*, and the second is *empowerment*. When you leave victimhood and move into empowerment, you start to elevate your thinking. Victims don't think that they can change their lives, make a difference, or have more money. Victims don't think that there are solutions to their problems, or to world problems. People who are empowered do.

When you move into the second stage of awakening, you start to wonder, "How can I solve these problems?" or, "How can I bring money into my life?" or, "How can I attract more wealth into my career?" You start to ask different questions and get different results. Elevating your thinking is partially thinking in terms of possibility.

Go back to the "What if Up?" game. Instead of thinking it's impossible to attract money, you start asking the very different and much more empowering questions such as "How can I think to attract money?", or, "What can I do to attract money?", or, "Where will money come to me in unexpected ways?" You elevate your thinking to the extent where you are no longer bouncing off circumstances or reacting to other people or events. You are now coming from a place where you are in charge of your own wealth. You are in charge of what's coming to you, because you've elevated your thinking to see a wider perspective.

One time I went to visit a relative in Ohio, and he was marveling at my wealth: my estate, my car collection, my guitar collection, and all the other bells and whistles that I have. He looked at me and said, "I could never have what you have." I was stunned by that, because that's not how I think anymore. I did at one point, but I elevated my thinking.

I looked at him and said, "Why can't you have any of this?" In his mind, because he was working a nine-to-five job with an hourly wage, success was not possible for him. When he looked around, he said, "I have a job, and I have a paycheck," but he doesn't see past these. He doesn't see other possibilities. I thought, "If you elevate your thinking, become more of an entrepreneur, and learn these secrets to attracting money, you can have what I have or even more."

I learned long time ago from my friend Bob Proctor that when money comes to you, it's not coming from your job; it's coming *through* your job. The money you attract isn't necessarily coming from where you think it's coming from. If you have a job and think, "I'm only going to make so much money from that job," you're forgetting that the universe can provide all kinds of new doors and windows for you to receive money through; your job is only one of them. By elevating your thinking, you say, "Money can come to me in any number of ways."

A long time ago, when I first heard about this concept, I thought, "How is that possible? I'm only an author. It can only come to me from my books." I dismissed the idea that I could be in movies, that I could have audios and videos, that I could be on the speaking circuit, that I could invent products that would make me a great deal of money. My mind was closed down and saw only one little pinhole of possibility.

In secret eight, you elevate your thinking to understand that money can come to you from a vast, surprising, unexpected, and unpredictable number of ways.

## PROBLEMS CREATE OPPORTUNITIES

Finally, secret number nine: *problems create opportunities*. One of my favorite people on the planet is marketing personality Donny Deutsch. Donny says, "Wherever you look around and see that somebody has a problem, or you have a problem, that's a moneymaking opportunity." If you look around and say, "Gosh, I wish somebody would do something about this," or, "I wish somebody would create a service to handle this particular problem," or, "I wish somebody would solve this particular dilemma," you've just given yourself a big signal for a moneymaking opportunity. Wherever you hear a problem, that's a dollar sign. That's secret number nine: learning to see problems as opportunities.

## ENDING POVERTY

I want to share an insight I've had about how people relate to money. I thought of it when I came up with the idea to create Operation Yes! I asked, how would I be able to help people stop foreclosures? How could I help somebody who's on the streets get back on their feet? I realized that there are three ways to stop poverty, foreclosures, and homelessness. All of them directly tie into attracting more money.

The first way is to improve your self-esteem, what I call *your level of deservingness*. When I was homeless, I felt worthless. I had low self-esteem and a low self-image. I thought that I wasn't worth much and didn't deserve much. My energy and self-love were incredibly low. I think anybody who's trying to attract money needs to improve their self-esteem and their level of deservingness. How do you do that?

First, you forgive yourself. When I looked at the fact that I was homeless, I had to say to myself, "Joe, you were doing the very best you knew how to do." All of us are doing the very best we know how to do. If we knew any better, we would have done something different.

Then decide "I am OK. I deserve better. I can love myself." You can love yourself, and you need to. Receiving or attracting more money begins with this first step: knowing you deserve it.

If any limiting beliefs kick in, such as, "I'll just waste the money," or "No, I don't really deserve it," you have to cleanse and release them. Maybe you can do it by being a little bit of a Socrates and asking yourself, "Does it really serve me not to believe I deserve anything? Does it really serve me to believe that I'm not worth anything?"

I believe that you're worth it; I believe that I'm worth it.

I've discovered that the more I can allow great wealth to come into my life, the more I can help everybody around me. If you want a great reason for becoming wealthy, for attracting money, realize that wealthy people can make a difference in the world. This is one of the most powerful reasons for attracting money.

If you really care about Third World countries, poverty, homelessness, or any issue that's out there, become wealthy. Attract money into your life. When you have bigger, more noble causes, you start to think, "I am worth it. I do deserve it. Yes, I do love myself."

This first step, again, is to improve your self-esteem, your level of deservingness. It can be as simple as saying to yourself, "I love myself. I deserve more."

The second step is to learn the law of attraction. Learn that when you focus on something, you tend to attract it. It's a basic law of psychology: whatever you focus on tends to expand. If you've been focusing on being broke or in debt, you were probably expanding the debt and making it even deeper. When you start to focus on attracting money, feeling wealthy, and feeling grateful for the wealth that you have, you kick in the law of attraction in a positive way.

The third step is to become an entrepreneur: gain an entrepreneurial mindset. You don't necessarily have to open your own business, but you can, for example write an e-book or create any number of digital video or audio products, which can be sold online.

My belief is everybody has something unique about them. It could be experience. It could be education. It could be a hobby. It could be a talent. It could be a pastime that you enjoy that other people might like to know how to do as well. You can turn any of those things into an information product.

Thinking like an entrepreneur empowers you. It enables you to start thinking, "I can create a business," or, "I can turn a problem into a moneymaking opportunity simply by turning on my inner radar, by seeing things differently." I'll tell you some stories about how I've done that and how others have done that.

Those are the three steps for stopping poverty. Those are the three steps that I'm using in Operation Yes!

1. Improve self-esteem and your level of deservingness.
2. Implement the law of attraction.
3. Think like an entrepreneur, have an entrepreneurial mindset, and quit giving your power away to the outside world. Instead, own it and use it within yourself.

## EMULATE THE SUCCESSFUL

Very wealthy people, such as Warren Buffett and Sam Walton, have these characteristics. They're relentless. They're fearless. They're focused. All of these are available to you.

Relentlessness is one—the capacity for persistence. It's within you; you call it forth from within your own gut. You can bring this courage forth from within yourself by calling on it.

The second characteristic is fearlessness. Billionaires and tycoons don't pay attention to the crowd. They pay attention to the inside of themselves. They have an inner compass. You have an inner compass as well. When you listen to it and follow it, you go in the direction of manifesting and attracting great wealth.

Warren Buffett has said that he does the opposite of what the crowd does. If the crowd is fearing the stock market, he does the opposite: he invests in the stock market. By being fearless about your dreams, about your goals, about wanting to attract more money, you can summon up more courage, energy, and persistence than you ever thought possible.

Then there's the characteristic of being focused. These tycoons have focused on their end result, the thing they want to accomplish. Sam Walton, for example, was very focused on making his stores the best ones available to the common person, and he created an empire that's still around today.

People like Warren Buffett, Sam Walton, or any others that you might name, possess relentlessness, persistence, fearlessness, and a focused mindset. All these things are available to you.

## THE SUPERMAN SYNDROME

Let me tell you how to incorporate these qualities in your own mindset right now. My friend Gene Landrum is another very wealthy man. He created the Chuck E. Cheese pizza chain. He's also written numerous books. One is called *The Superman Syndrome*. Basically, he says, "If you pretend to have the characteristics of the people you admire, you actually call forth those characteristics from within you."

Gene says to pretend there's a great big S on your chest. It's under your clothes, so nobody else can see it, but you know it's there. It means you are Superman or Superwoman. It means that you can pretend that you are already wealthy. You can pretend that you are already Warren Buffett or Sam Walton. When you pretend that you are this particular person, you pretend to think like them. You pretend to act like them. You go in the direction of becoming them.

This doesn't mean that you copy these people or become clones of them. Rather, you're finding the aspects of these tycoons that you admire, and you are pushing a button in your brain to bring out the same characteristics within you.

You can do this right now. When you think about any tycoons that come to mind, what do you like about them? What traits do they have for attracting money? You might write it down in a notebook or journal. You might let it roll around in your mind for a little bit. As you focus on it, imagine that you now have that trait, even if you have to fake it until you make it, even if you have to pretend, even if this seems like an acting exercise right now.

What if you were the Superman of attracting money? How would you feel? How would you think? How would you act? Those are questions that you might want to answer maybe in your mind, maybe on paper. As you play with these qualities, you'll find yourself incorporating them, and very quickly, these will become a part of you.

These shared mindsets of wealthy people are available to you. They're not foreign. When we talk about being relentless or fearless or focused, those are not things that are not available to you. Those are not traits that are not already in you. What you want to do now is call them forth. You can do it by pretending you're already wealthy.

## USE YOUR MIND TO YOUR ADVANTAGE

Throughout this book, I've encouraged you to be aware of your mind, to be aware of how you're thinking. I've told you about the "What if Up?" game. Right now, play "What if Up?" Ask yourself, "What if what I'm learning right now is going to make me a money magnet? What if what I'm learning right now is going to cause unexpected income to come into my life in joyous, wonderful, surprising ways?"

This is how you use your mind to your best advantage: have an expectation for success. If you expect things to go poorly, you will look around and find evidence for that expectation. You have a belief that things won't work out. As you read the newspaper, watch TV, or overhear conversations, your mind will pick out the evidence that supports that belief and that expectation. I'm encouraging you to stop, to pause, take another look, and have a mindset that expects success.

You expect money to come into your life. You expect to attract money. When you do this, your mind starts to look for evidence to support this new reality. Reality, to me, is nothing but a belief-driven universe. It's made up of our mental constructs. When you believe or expect that money's coming to you in unforeseen ways, or you expect that you are now attracting money, you start looking for it. Instead of turning your mind toward the negative, it's turned toward the positive. This is a deep shift in perception. It happens with a choice. You flip the switch within yourself by deciding, "I am now attracting money. I wonder where the money will come from."

Instead of asking this in a worried way, you ask it in an expectant way. Right now, are you asking yourself, "I wonder where that money will come from?" meaning that you don't think money is going to show up, or are you asking yourself, "I wonder where that money will come from," meaning you are waiting for it curiously and expectantly? You know it's going to come, but you don't know how.

It's a little bit like buying a new car. When you first think about buying it, you notice the same model on the road. Right after you buy it, there seems to be an invasion of the car you just bought.

Decades ago, I was considering buying a Saturn, I never saw them on the road, but after I bought one, I did. I saw them everywhere.

Why is that? My mind now expected to see them. My mind was on high alert to look for Saturns, only because I turned on the switch that says, "I'm now interested in Saturns."

You can do the same thing with money. You now expect money. You now attract money. You now look for the opportunities for money to show up, and you will find them. You will overhear opportunities in conversations. You will read about opportunities when you read the papers or books or listen to audios. They will show up in your awareness because of this new expectation. Again, you flip the switch by asking yourself, "What do I expect when it comes to money?" and choosing to expect to attract money easily and effortlessly.

## THE FIT-A-RITA

Let me tell you a story of how this works, especially in terms of turning a problem into a moneymaking opportunity. For many years, I entered a lot of different bodybuilding contests. Bill Phillips had one called the Body for Life contest. I entered it nine different times and completed it seven times. I got an honorable mention one time. During the training, I was very strict about eating, dieting, drinking, and working out. I was very focused on achieving a healthy, fit body and losing a lot of weight.

I managed to succeed, but it was a sacrifice. Once when I was out for dinner with friends, everybody was ordering margaritas. I was drinking ice water. I didn't want to have a margarita, because the average margarita has anywhere from three hundred to a thousand calories in it.

I was frustrated. I slammed my fist on the table and said, "What we need is a bodybuilder's margarita!"

Everybody laughed, but I saw an opportunity. The light bulb went on over my head, and I thought, "Wait a minute. I could create that. I could create a fitness margarita, a bodybuilding margarita." I knew it was possible.

This is how you find opportunities. Somebody states a problem; in this case, it was me. The next day, I contacted a doctor I know. I told him about my idea. He laughed a little, but he thought it was a good idea. He put me in touch with a nutritionist. At first, he scoffed at the idea, but he did a little research and thought, "Wait a minute. Maybe there's actually a market for a healthy margarita."

The three of us teamed up. We went through a bunch of experiments. We made different batches. We ended up with an all-natural, all-healthy, sugar-free, six-calorie margarita. We ended up calling it the Fit-a-Rita. It has no carbs in it, six calories, no sugar, and all natural ingredients. It's sweetened with stevia. You can turn a simple packet into a full-fledged, all-natural margarita with just a little water and a little tequila.

I began to market Fit-a-Rita. I signed a deal with a company that wanted to sell it to the Latino market. Eventually I got an offer from a company that wanted eleven million packets of Fit-a-Rita.

This was big money, and it came from being frustrated, slamming my first down on the table, and saying, "Why doesn't somebody come up with a healthy margarita?" In this case, I was the answer, and I'm the one attracting money because of it.

This is how you turn your mind on to expecting and attracting money. You see a problem as an opportunity. When you expect to attract money, when you expect to turn problems into opportunities, you start to see them. They start to become apparent. Other people might overlook them, but your eyes and ears and mind are now turned on. Maybe you too one day can create something like Fit-a-Rita, or something even better.

We've covered a lot of ground here. I want to encourage you to integrate everything you've learned from this chapter by writing out the questions, doing the belief clearing process, and letting all of it settle into the new you.

As you go through this material, you are rewiring your brain to attract and expect money. This is a great experience and a great feeling. I'm excited for you, because I don't know when the light is going to turn on for you. It might be right after you finish this chapter, it might be while you're reading the next chapter, but money is coming to you right now.

# FOUR
# EXPLODING MONEY MYTHS

There are a lot of myths about money. These are the results of a cultural trance that many people have fallen into. They can block you from attracting money into your life. Let's clear them up right now.

## THE WORLD IS IN DANGER

The first myth, which many people believe, is that the world is in financial danger and that we are at the mercy of the stock market, banks, and other financial institutions. The truth of the matter is, you do not have to react or respond to the perceived chaos out there in the world.

I've already mentioned the stages of awakening. The first one is victimhood. Most of us stay in victimhood. Most of us react to world events. If we buy into our reactions when we see the stock market dropping, we get nervous. If you think like Warren Buffett, you think there's an opportunity. I would suggest that Warren Buffett is not coming from the mindset of being a victim; he's coming from an empowered mindset. That's where you need to be in order to attract money. You want to feel empowered. You don't want to feel like a victim.

Although I encourage you not to watch the news, if you do, pay attention to how you feel. If you let these messages seep in when you hear about the stock market, banks, or other financial institutions doing one thing or another, notice how you feel. Do you feel good? Does your energy go up? Do you go into a panic mode? Do you feel confident? Most of the time, the news will make you feel horrible. When you feel horrible about how you're perceiving the world, you don't know what your choices are. You don't know what your next actions should be. You're walking blindly through life.

If you come from a mindset of empowerment, you see the opportunities; you see the choices. You know what's right for you to do next.

It doesn't matter what the world is doing. In reality, we don't know what the world is doing anyway. It's being reported by the media, which are only giving you snapshots of the worst-case scenarios; they're not giving you the entire picture. In order for you to attract money, you must come from your heart. You must come from a trusting place. You must come from an empowered place.

## IF YOU PROSPER, OTHERS WILL LOSE

Another common myth is that if you prosper, others will lose. Prosperity means that you may not be evolved; you may not be spiritual. That's a horrible myth, because it causes you to shut down your own good and block your wealth from coming into your life. I've found that the more money I bring into my life, the more spiritual and evolved I am, the more I can help others prosper.

The more prosperous you become, the more you can help others prosper. You can help yourself. You can help your family, your friends, your community, the country, the planet. You can fund or establish good causes.

If you really want to make a difference in the world, start by making a difference in one person's prosperity—yours. When you do, you find that money is a very highly evolved spiritual tool. In and of itself, it doesn't mean anything, but you can use it with awareness, consciousness, and spirituality to make a difference in healing this planet. It is good, it is holy, it is spiritual to attract money.

## MONEY IS DANGEROUS

Another myth says that money and power are dangerous; they change people, making them arrogant, self-centered, greedy, and power-hungry. But you can certainly look around and find examples of people who have become arrogant, self-centered, greedy, or power hungry with or without money. You can also find people who have obtained a great deal of money and are not arrogant, self-centered, greedy, or power-hungry.

Money by itself is nothing. We provide the meaning to it. Are you providing a meaning to money that says it's a useful tool, or are you providing a meaning that says it's a poison? You have a choice. I've repeatedly emphasized that you want to choose higher awareness. You want to choose a more empowered way of thinking and being. The more money you have, the more you can make a difference in the world. Money is not dangerous. Money is actually wonderful.

## IT'S TOO EASY

Another myth out there is that attracting wealth by simply visualizing and feeling it is too easy. It's a hoax. I want to laugh at that one, because the skeptics who say that don't realize the deeper aspect of visualization and feeling the end result of what you want.

Some people think that money will come if they just sit, visualize, and feel it. They don't know that they also have to take the other steps. There's also the law of right action. It isn't enough to just sit, visualize, and feel money. At some point you have get up and do something. You have to act on your ideas. You have to make the phone calls, send out the letters or résumés, answer the ad, open the business, buy the book, or attend the seminar. You have to do something.

I've also pointed out that the more you remove the unconscious blocks and limitations within you, the easier it is to attract money, even by just sitting and visualizing. I think visualizing is powerful, but I want you to do it in the way I've described it: Nevillize your visualization; imagine the end result of attracting the money you've been seeking. When you do that, you accelerate the process of manifesting it. You must also take action. The law of right action is right behind the law of attraction. They work together.

People who say that visualizing and feeling wealth is a hoax don't understand how all of this works. You know now. You now know that visualization and feeling and Nevillizing work, but you have to take part in the process by taking action.

## BUSINESSWOMEN ARE TOO DRIVEN

Another common myth is that women who do well in business are too driven or too difficult and do not care enough for their families. I don't buy that one at all. I think women who are motivated by their hearts will have more time and money and will find greater balance between home life and business.

This goes back to the law of expectation. If you expect to find women with money who are not happy, who are driven or difficult and don't care about their families, you will look around and find examples of that. However, if you believe that there are women out there who are motivated by their hearts and who have enough time and money, you will look around and find the Mary Kays of the world. You will find examples to back up your belief and your expectation.

Yes, there are examples of both out there, but you want to focus on the model for you. Whom do you want to be like? Whom do you want to emulate? What characteristics do you want to have? When you focus on those qualities, you draw them out from within you.

I think you can be an inspiration to the rest of the world. It doesn't matter if you can find examples of women or men who are too focused on money or too driven. What matters is that you find in yourself the example of somebody who is whole and balanced and wealthy and happy. That's how you handle this myth.

## YOU CAN'T HAVE IT ALL

Another myth is that you can't have it all; you are doomed to failure if you think you can have a great career, lots of money, plenty of recreation time, and a wonderful personal life. If you hold on to that belief, you will create that very doom for yourself.

In other words, people who feel like victims have given up. The statements "You can't have it all," "You're doomed to failure if you think you can have a great career, lots of money, and a great home life," are coming straight from a victim mentality. This is somebody who has tried but didn't try successfully. They tried and failed, and they did not try again.

The great secret of life is not that you've tried; it's that you keep on trying. Many times the things I've worked on—business ideas or books—didn't turn out the way I wanted. I did not stop. I did not give up. I went on to the next thing.

Years ago, when I was homeless on the streets of Dallas, if I believed that I was doomed to failure, that I was doomed to never have money, to never have a wonderful life, I would not be here today. This again is a choice. I say give up being a victim. Go on to the next stage of awakening and become empowered. Trust yourself. Trust tomorrow. Trust hope. Trust the actions you're taking. Trust me with what I'm teaching you in this book.

## WE HAVE CREATED A WORLD OF EXCESS

Another myth is that we have created a world of excess and anger. We are now experiencing that energy in our weather, our financial struggles, our ecological challenges, and so forth. We have created a dark world that will fall, and we'll suffer the consequences.

Again, this is coming from a victim mentality. The truth is that as human beings, we are evolving faster than ever before. When you come from an empowered mindset, you realize that you are becoming more and more conscious. As you become more conscious, you can trust that we are moving forward and upward in a positive direction. We are creating a more abundant world. Maybe we can't accurately describe it yet, because it's still unfolding, but you and I are becoming financially safe and financially free, and we will all prosper as long as we play out our piece of the music. As long as you look within, find your part of the puzzle, and act on it, you are helping to create a new world based on happiness, spirituality, prosperity, abundance, and most of all love. All of this happens from letting go of fear.

## FEAR VERSUS TRUST

If you think about all the different myths that I've been talking about here, what they have in common is the one word *fear*. If you think about all the answers I've given to these myths, you can come up with the answer: *trust*.

Here's your choice: are you going to come from fear, or are you going to come from faith? Are you going to come from intimidation by the media, negativity, gossip, the victim mentality? You have a choice. I, for one, want to come from faith. I want to come from trust. I want to come from love. I can choose to go back and become a victim, but once you've tasted empowerment, you will never go back, because you realize it would be insane. We are on this journey of awakening, you and I together, and we can make this planet the abundant place we want it to be as long as we listen to our music and fulfill our song. I'm encouraging you to do that now.

## YOUR MONEY BIOGRAPHY

At this point I want to offer you an awakening process. I'm going to ask you to write out two different scenarios. The first one is your money biography. In other words, I'd like you to write out how you learned about money. In my particular case, as I was growing up in Ohio, I remember learning that there wasn't enough money. My father and mother had a lot of fights about it. I heard the phrase, "Money does not grow on trees." I heard that we were so desperate for money, if not outright poor, that my father would tell us only to use so much toilet paper, so much toothpaste, so much food. He would look at the receipts when my mother came home from shopping. He would fight with her if he thought she had spent too much.

There's more depth to this. When you write out your money biography, I want you to fully explore how you feel about it based on what you learned when you were growing up. Maybe you heard the same expression I did: money doesn't grow on trees. Maybe you concluded, as I did, that there's never enough: you had to work hard for the money, and even then you'd realize it wasn't enough to survive, let alone enable you to do what you wanted.

This is your money biography. I'd like you to spend a few minutes writing it out in order to become aware of the beliefs that have been circulating in your brain. For the most part, they have made up the programming that has caused you either to attract or repel money. Until now, you've probably pushed it away and didn't even know you were doing it. Now, as you're changing your mind and rewiring your own brain, you'll start to attract money.

I want to streamline the process. I want to take away all the blocks and snags. I want you to be able to have money coming into you easily and effortlessly, without any snags whatsoever. The first way to do this is to become aware of your money mentality. When you have a chance, write out your money biography.

The second part of this process is to write a new money biography. I want you to completely rewrite your script, your biography of how you learned about money. How would you prefer to have been introduced to money?

In my new biography, I would write down that my father was able to make money easily and effortlessly from his ideas, from his work, from things he enjoyed doing. I learned that money was available to all of us, everybody in my family, my friends, my neighbors, the city, the community. All we had to do was ask for it, take a few actions to bring it into our lives, and there it was. I did learn that money did grow on trees. Maybe metaphorically, but there it was. It wasn't hard to get. I did learn that money was always there for me. Whenever I wanted something, whether it was a book or a toy or a vacation, the money was there—more than enough of it. I've had a great relationship with money ever since I was born, and I still have a great relationship with it. In fact, we're the best of friends. Money loves me, and I love money.

As I was talking about how I became introduced to money, I felt a little down. I was reexperiencing all of the unhappiness and discomfort. When I went through the second scenario and described how I wish it had been, my energy went up. My happiness went up. A little smile appeared on my face. My heart started to warm a little bit more. I actually started to feel even better about money. This is the power of this process.

Here's the great secret: what took place in your past is very vague. There are studies that show that we don't remember the past accurately; we hardly remember it at all. In fact, we get it wrong almost 98 percent of the time, according to one study I read. Our mind is projecting our beliefs onto our past, and we think it's real. But the past is gone.

If the past is largely fictitious, it can be rewritten. By writing out how you thought you were brought up about money, you become aware of these limitations, and you release them. By writing out how you want to feel about money, you install new programming; you install new scripts. Do this as soon as you have a chance.

## SEVERAL SPIRITUAL WAYS TO ATTRACT MONEY

I have a real treat for you at this point: spiritual ways to attract money. These are some of my all-time favorite ways to pull in money easily and effortlessly. They are simple and easy to do. Maybe you've heard of one or two, but you probably haven't heard of all seven. They have worked for me. They have passed the test of time. They have helped me go from nothing to multimillions of dollars. These are my seven spiritual ideas for attracting money.

## 1. CARRY A $100 BILL

Carry a $100 bill in your pocket. The first time I heard that, I did not have a $100 bill; I don't think I had ever seen one at that point. I might have had $1, $5, $20 bills; maybe I had seen a $50 bill. But I heard that if you carry a $100 bill in your pocket, you'll start to feel more prosperous.

I had to save up. When I finally had $100, I went to the bank and said, "I want to turn this into a $100 bill." I took the bill, put it in my pocket, and started thinking about money more. I started to think I was just a wee bit more prosperous than I was when I was carrying only a few dollars. I'd go through my day imagining what I would spend the $100 for.

I didn't spend the money; I pretended I was spending it. Occasionally, I would break the bill, but as soon as I could, I would replenish it with another $100 bill. I did this for years. Over time, I got to the point where I was adding other $100 bills to the first one. Over more time, I realized I was no longer using any money out of my wallet; I was leaving the $100 bills in it. I would reach into my front pocket and pull out a money clip whenever I needed to buy something.

The first tip, and it's so easy to do, is to carry a $100 bill. Again, this was not an overnight thing for me. It probably took a few weeks to get started. Maybe you can do it today. If you can, please do so. For me, this is a no-brainer way of keeping a prosperity mindset.

## 2. GIVE AWAY $1 A DAY

This idea came to me from a friend of mine named Todd Silva. Todd's a wonderful person. He was my guitar teacher in Houston. He came up with the idea of giving away $1 a day. Just take a $1 bill every day and slip it somewhere where somebody will find it. Do not give it to anyone in particular—a waiter, waitress, or somebody on the corner—unless you really feel compelled to.

Todd's theory is that when you plant this money to surprise somebody later, you're actually engaging your own sense of prosperity. When you start to imagine, "I wonder who will find it?", "I wonder what they'll think?", "I wonder what they'll do with it?", you'll open a playfulness within yourself that attracts more money. You take off the edge around money as being something that's hard to get. By giving it away, you're suggesting to yourself that it's easy to let money go and it's easy to let money come.

Todd's movement to give a dollar away every day is picking up speed. He has a website for it. He sends out a newsletter every Monday or Tuesday. He encourages people to take a dollar out of their wallet or purse. Slip it inside a book. Leave it under a tray or a plate. Leave it someplace for somebody else to find.

## 3. PRAY

I've never talked about the third step, but I have to say from my heart that it has been a turning point in my life. I'm talking about praying: asking for help from a higher power. Yes, you can call it God—whatever that higher power is for you.

When I was in Houston and I had a lot of bills, I'd lie in bed and I'd look over to my roll-top desk; the bills were stacked up on top of it. I'd look at them and say, "I have no idea how to pay these. I have no idea where the money's going to come from." I'd pray. I'd get silent, and I'd say out loud, "God, I need your help. I don't know how to pay that stack of bills. I don't know where I'm going to get the money. I don't know what to do next, so I'm turning it over to you."

This praying was done in secret. I didn't tell other people about it, but it was a turning point, because somehow, some way, the money always came. Those bills got paid every time, usually before they were due, and to such an extent that that house was paid for, the cars that I was worried about were paid for. All the bills, for food, clothing, whatever, were paid. I'm now at a new level of prosperity and income that is staggering, almost unimaginable to the Joe that was lying in bed, praying for help back in those Houston days.

When you pray, you're asking for help from a higher power, something wiser than you. Even if you happen to be an atheist, you can consider that when you're praying, you're speaking out loud to a vaster part of your own unconscious mind. Your conscious mind can't see all of your opportunities and your possibilities, but your unconscious mind can. When you're praying, you're calling out loud to something wiser and bigger than you to come in and save the day. It could be your unconscious mind. For me, it's the divine, and this is a very spiritual approach to attracting money.

## 4. SCRIPT OUT HOW TO ATTRACT MONEY

The fourth spiritual idea for attracting money is to script out how you would love to attract money. Write out a Nevillized script, in which you describe how you've attracted money in some unexpected way and how it feels. You get into the emotion of it. It's probably thrilling.

You can do this right now, either in writing or mentally. Ask, what would it feel like if $100,000 fell into your lap? What would it feel like if $50,000 in cash were suddenly sitting beside you on the seat? It doesn't matter where it came from. How would you feel? Get into the emotion of it. Would you be smiling? Would you feel joyful? Would your heart beat a little faster? Would you feel a sense of ecstasy? Maybe you're curious. Maybe you're in wonderment. Scripting with emotion helps attract more money to you.

Now you can do this in your mind, you can speak it out loud, but it's far more powerful if you write it out. When you write out anything, you are communicating with your unconscious mind. You're putting your thoughts on paper. As you read them, they go back into your unconscious mind through your eyes. Writing these feelings down is far more powerful than just visualizing or thinking. When you have a chance, script out an experience of attracting money in some joyous, wonderful way.

## 5. CREATE A VISION BOARD

The fifth spiritual idea for attracting money is to create a vision board. Sometimes it's called a treasure map. You're creating the life you would love to have. Imagine taking a great big piece of poster board. It's all white. Clip out images and symbols that symbolize abundance and wealth to you and paste them on your vision board. It could be a new car that you've been dreaming about. It could be a new house, a new set of clothes or shoes. It could be numbers in a bank account. You could put up photos of money—$100, $50, $20 bills. Put what you would love to bring into your life on this vision board.

Your mind works with emotion and symbols. If you create a vision board that has symbols with emotional meaning to you, you will communicate directly with your unconscious mind, and it will magnetize you to attract the things represented on your vision board.

## 6. CELEBRATE WHAT YOU'VE ACCOMPLISHED

The sixth spiritual idea for attracting money is to celebrate what you've already done. Too many of us—and I've been this way myself—have become workaholics; we just keep our nose to the grindstone. We keep pushing and pushing and clawing and clawing. We have to take time to acknowledge what we've done.

I've created a playday for myself: once a week (admittedly sometimes it's once a month), I'll take the day off, get in one of my cars, and drive to another city. I'll do something that's fun for me. More often than not, it means visiting a bookstore. I admit I'm a bookaholic. I love books. I write books. I read books. I give books. I review books. Going to bookstores is very relaxing for me. It's a way to reward myself. I also lie in my hot tub almost every night—a very relaxing thing for me to do. It's a reward, an acknowledgment.

For you, it might mean taking a little time off, seeing a movie, going to a museum, having a nice dinner, buying a piece of clothing, doing some shopping, going for a walk in nature, taking a hike, or going for a bike ride.

You have to celebrate what you've been doing. The fact that you've invested in this book and reading it means that you should pause and celebrate. You should acknowledge what you've been doing.

This is a way to raise your deservingness. This is a way to tell yourself that you are doing well and you're proud of yourself. It improves your self-image and your self-esteem. Celebrate what you've done, even if it's a small thing. Go out and do something for you. It could even be very small, like walking around the block and getting fresh air, taking a bath, or having a nice dinner. Do something that feels good to you and for you.

## 7. PROSPEROUS PURCHASING

The seventh spiritual idea for attracting money is one of my all-time favorites. I call it *prosperous purchasing*. Prosperous purchasing means that every now and then, when you feel that inner nudge to buy something, even if it might be a little pricey, you go ahead and do it. You do it because it's a vote for abundance. It's a vote for prosperity. You are telling yourself that you deserve it and you can afford it.

One time I bought a $700 gold lighter. I smoke cigars from time to time. I had given a workshop one night. I had sold out of all of my product at a display that I had at this event, and I wanted to reward myself.

I went to a cigar store. I walked in and roamed around. They had a lot of lighters there, and I asked the owner. I said, "If someone walked in here and said he wanted the best lighter in the house, what would you show him?" He showed me a $700 gold-plated Dupont lighter, and I bought it. I bought it to anchor the good feelings. Now this is important: I wasn't buying a $700 lighter merely to buy a $700 lighter. I was buying it to anchor the prosperity I had already received and to reward myself for it.

When you see something that you want to buy and you can afford it, go ahead and do it as an acknowledgment of you and your own prosperity.

Note that I said, if you can afford to buy it. I'm not encouraging you to go into debt. I'm not encouraging you to go crazy. I'm not encouraging you to borrow money. But if you have the money and you see something, go ahead and buy it. This is prosperous purchasing.

Once in San Diego, I created and held an event called "The Miracles Weekend." During my stay, I went to look at some cars. I spotted a Rolls-Royce Phantom, one of the most luxurious and expensive cars in the world, which had a price tag of about $400,000. I drove that car over a three-day period. I kept going back to the car dealership and kept thinking about that car. I realized that by sitting in that luxurious, handmade Rolls-Royce Phantom, my abundance IQ went up, my prosperity feeling went up, my sense of deservingness went up. I decided I had to buy that car. I did. I bought a $400,000 car for $325,000 and brought it home.

Before you judge me for spending that much money on a car, let me tell you what happened. It will happen to you when you start prosperous purchasing.

It wasn't more than a day after owning that car that I had the idea for a Rolls-Royce Phantom Master Mind. As I've already explained, a Master Mind is when two or more people get together to support each other in going for their dreams. I wondered if anybody would pay to sit in the Phantom and have a Master Mind with me. I decided to charge $5,000 per person.

I would see if two people would sit in the back of the Rolls. I would be in the front and I'd have a coauthor, a business partner, with me to accompany me, so it would be four of us. I sent the announcement out to my email list. To my amazement, the first Rolls-Royce Phantom Master Mind sold out instantly. I had to announce a second one. It sold out instantly. I hard to announce a third one. It too sold out, and I announced a fourth one.

Why did that happen? The idea for this money attracting idea came as a direct result of buying the car. The idea was not there before it; the idea came after it. This is prosperous purchasing.

As you go about your day, your shopping, or your wandering through catalogs and flipping through magazines, be aware of when you see something that seems to have this prosperity charge: you feel almost compelled to have it. You check within yourself to make sure you're not doing something crazy. You check your bankbook to make sure you have the money. I encourage you to purchase it, because it'll make you feel more prosperous. The more prosperous you feel, the more you'll be able to attract more money.

## THE ANGRY SQUIRREL

To end this chapter, let me talk about a couple of things. If you are in a position where you've lost a job, you're concerned about your next paycheck, or you're concerned about paying your bills, your rent, your food, or your health care, I feel for you. I want to remind you that this will pass. What you're experiencing is your current reality, but current reality will and always does change. Your experience right now is not set in stone. It's changing right now, because you are actually investing in your self by reading this material. You're learning how to attract money. Money is on its way to you.

I also want to remind you that when the world looks as if it's really chaotic and it's breaking up, that's actually good. It means that something new is being formed. It means something new is being restructured.

You are part of the process, and you are one of the pieces of the puzzle. When it all comes together and settles down and the clouds clear and the dust settles, you will realize, "It all makes sense now. Now I know what my next work, my next job, or my next business is. Now I see where the money is coming from."

Let me tell you a quick story about a squirrel. This squirrel tried to move into my attic. Of course I didn't want him there. I didn't want him moving his family and friends in, so I got him out of the attic. I plugged up the hole so he couldn't get back in. While I was plugging it up, his world was chaotic. He was unhappy. He threw a fit. He threw acorns at the house. He would hang from the screen and swear at me, but he didn't know that I had actually built a beautiful squirrel house for him right beside my house up in the trees. This was made with enough room that he could move in family, friends, and a stereo system if he wanted.

The squirrel didn't see it right away. All he saw was the panic. All he saw was the chaos. All he saw was that his life was breaking up around him and his security was gone. When he finally found the house that I put up in the trees for him, he went to it gleefully. He's moved into it. He has a wonderful life with his family in his new home.

You are probably much like the squirrel. Right now it seems crazy. You don't know where your next paycheck's coming from. You don't know where the next job is coming from, but the wonderful thing is that this experience is forcing you to look at doing something different. Most people go through their lives living out their patterns, doing the same thing over and over until something stops them. Right now, the world at large may have stopped you, but it's only to get you to pause, reflect, regroup, and do something different. This is your moment. This is your chance. The sun always comes up again. The sun is rising for you right now. Do the exercises I've been giving you. Expect money to come into your life. Expect success, and you will find it.

# FIVE
## SHORTCUTS TO ATTRACTING MONEY

In this chapter, we're going to talk about shortcuts to attracting money. To begin with, the biggest, the greatest, the most profound shortcut that I can tell you is this one: be happy now.

Everybody wants to attract more wealth, more health, more success. We all have a long list of things we want to attract, but what are we really wanting? When you say you want more money, aren't you saying that you want it for a particular reason? Aren't you thinking, "If I have more money, I'll be able to buy more clothes; I'll be able to buy more food; I'll be able to pay my bills; I'll be able to have a bigger home"?

What are you really after when you say any of those things? When you say, "I want to attract more money to have more success," aren't you really saying that when you have success, you have a feeling of having arrived?

I'm inviting you to dig deeper into your want. When you say, "I want to attract money," you want it for a particular feeling. You want to be able to say, "I have arrived. I am happy. I am finally there."

In a way, this is a grand illusion. You're creating monkeys, and you're chasing them down the street. Whenever you catch a monkey, another one starts running, and you start chasing it. These monkeys are your desires. They are causing you to go crazy and constantly feeling unhappy with yourself.

The great secret to attracting more money right now is to feel happy right now. When you settle into this moment, you're no longer concerned about the past. You're no longer worried about the future. You're right here, you're right now, in this moment. You have abundance. You have wealth. You have what you've secretly been wanting all along.

You've been telling yourself, "When I have more money, I will be happy. When I have the house, I will be happy. When I have the job, I will be happy. When I have the car, I will be happy. When I have fill in the blank, I will be happy."

Life doesn't work that way. The law of attraction doesn't work that way. This is probably the most breakthrough-oriented principle that I could share with you: when you take a deep breath and you realize that all is OK and you are OK in this moment, you actually create a new vibrational signal. It goes out from you in this moment to attract the very things you've been wanting all along.

The formula you've been using is to be unhappy now and go after something that you think will make you happy. In the process of chasing it, you're generally very unhappy. If you achieve it one day, you're happy for a moment, and then you go through the process again.

Being unhappy, chasing something else, maybe being happy for a moment when you achieve it, then being unhappy and going through the process again—that process doesn't work. This is wonderful news, because you can change the process simply by changing your mind. You change your mind by looking around and saying, "This moment is actually great. I can be happy in this moment."

When you are happy now, you finally have achieved what you thought money would bring: happiness. When you are happy now, you are able to clearly see your next steps to manifesting money in your life. When you come from this place of security—of not needing security—you actually start to attract the money that will give you the security you've been longing for. It all begins and ends with being happy now.

How do you get there? How do you move into this place of being now, when your rent's due, you're out of work, or your belly is hungry and you're really needing to eat? How do you find that place of happiness in this moment?

You can do a couple of things. One is to be aware that the past is gone and the future will never arrive. When you think about the past, you do it *now*. Your thinking is very inaccurate. You're conjuring up images and memories in this moment, and you're calling it the past.

When you think about the future, you're projecting ahead, but you're doing it in this moment. When you start thinking about the past or the future, you've deceived yourself, because in reality there's only now. You can only be in the now; you can mentally distract yourself with thoughts, but the point of power is for you to be in the now. You can return to this moment with awareness, with consciousness. That's the first thing: to remind yourself of how you are thinking so that you can bring yourself into this moment.

## FEEL GRATITUDE

The second thing you can do is to feel gratitude. I've already talked about the power of gratitude. It's probably the single most powerful force that you can use. It costs you nothing, and you can begin to use it right this second by looking around and saying, "I am grateful for . . ." and mentioning something you're sincerely grateful for. It could be this book, the car you're driving, the seat you're sitting in. You could be grateful for somebody—even a pet. There's something in your life you're genuinely grateful for. When you move into this moment and start to feel gratitude now, you change your internal signal. You start to send out a vibe that's coming from this moment to attract more things and experiences to be grateful for, including more money.

## FORGIVE

The third thing you can do to bring yourself into this moment is to forgive. I've talked about forgiveness, but this is so important and so profound that it's worth mentioning at least one more time. When you forgive, you release stuck energy. This energy isn't stuck in the past; it's not stuck in the future; it's stuck in you right this moment.

There are countless stories of prisoners of war who reach a place in their minds where they can forgive their tormentors. That's profound. You probably don't have to forgive at that deep a level, but you need to forgive yourself, your family, your friends, your employers—anybody you're holding a grudge against—and most importantly yourself.

When you forgive yourself, you open up a flow of love that brings you back to your point of power, which, as I keep saying, is now. Again, what you really want when you say, "I want to attract money," is happiness. You simply think, "When I have money, I will be happy." You can be happy now. It's a decision. When you're happy now, you can see with greater clarity your options to attract more money through the law of right action. It all begins, it all ends, with now. Be here now.

## BREATHING

You may be in a position where you're aching, hurting for money, and it's very difficult for you to even read the statement, "Be happy now." You're feeling, "I'm desperate. I must have money. I need it by Friday. I need it by next week." I understand that feeling; I've been there; I remember it well. You have to take the edge off. You have to remove the desperate feeling. As long as you're feeling desperate, you will send out an energy of desperation that will revisit experiences of desperation. You have to break that pattern.

You can do this by taking a deep breath, focusing on what you're grateful for in this moment, smiling, thinking of happy memories, forgiving everybody involved in whatever you have been resentful for, and bringing yourself into this moment.

There are some other techniques as well; I've used them in my own life in times of high stress, when I really wondered where the money was coming from and how I was going to pay the bills.

The first one is breathing. Take in a slow, deep breath, hold it, and then release it as you're counting, say, to eight. Slowly, one, two, three, four, five, six, seven, eight. As you are taking in a slow breath and holding it and releasing it to the count of eight, you calm yourself down.

This is important. Your stress, your frustration, your desperation, your worrying will not help you attract money. You have to take the stress off by breathing slowly, easily, effortlessly. You calm yourself down. You bring yourself into the moment. Breathing is free. You can do it in any moment, and you can do it right now.

## YOU'RE REALLY OK

Another thing that I do to help take the stress off is remind myself that I'm in this moment. Most of the time, stress is about the future, not this moment. You're worried about next week, next month, or next year. You're worried about the next paycheck, but in this moment, everything is actually OK. Yes, you may want more money. Yes, you may have desires, but in this moment, you're actually fine. You're reading this book. You're able to breathe. Maybe you had something for lunch. You're alive and well. You're doing OK. Remind yourself of that.

Sometimes when I'm driving and I'm feeling a little nervous, I will reach over and caress the dashboard. I'll remind myself, "Be here now." Touching something physical right then helps bring me back into the moment.

If I'm at home, I might touch my car keys, or I might touch the chair I'm in. If I'm sitting at a table, I might rub the wooden table. I'm saying to myself, "I'm here now. It's OK. Just relax." I'll tie it into breathing. I'll take in a deep breath, hold it in, and count to eight as I release it slowly. I'm relaxing.

## THE TAPPING CURE

Another technique you can use is called EFT, which stands for *Emotional Freedom Techniques*. There's a movie out called *Try It on Everything*, which is well worth seeing (I actually appear in it). It describes and illustrates EFT so that anybody can use it. The film proves that EFT works by documenting people who have used it to go through high stress situations.

EFT is known as the tapping cure. It's like psychological acupuncture, because you're tapping on certain parts of your body while you're making certain statements. (For these body parts, see the accompanying diagram.) I use EFT almost every day. I can teach you to do it right now.

In EFT, you're taking a statement, usually a statement of concern, a fear, or some issue that you have. For our purposes, let's use money. Take a statement such as "I am worried about money"; "I am desperate about money"; "I am very concerned about where my money is coming from."

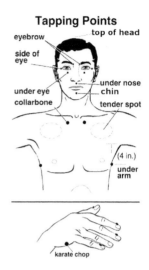

**Tapping Points**

1. Tap the underside of the karate chop part of your hand (see diagram) with the fingers of the other hand while saying to yourself something like, "Even though I'm worried about money, I deeply love, accept, and forgive myself."

2. Then you take the keyword "worried." Move to the top of your head, the crown area, and tap it a couple of times while saying, "Worried."

3. Gently tap above your eyebrows on the inside of your eyes, saying, "Worried."

4. Move to the far side of your eyes and say, "Worried," tapping.

5. Then underneath your eyes, tapping and saying, "Worried."

6. Then under your nose, right above your lip, in that little indention called the philtrum, tap and say, "Worried."

7. Underneath your lip, right above your chin, tap and say, "Worried."

8. Move to the left part of your chest. You'll find a little bit of a sore spot there. Tap or rub that area, saying, "Worried."

Then you repeat the procedure, this time using the statement, "Even though I'm worried about money, I deeply love and accept myself," again tapping on the areas that I've just outlined.

By doing this simple little process, you release the stress. You even release the belief itself. EFT has been used on a wide variety of beliefs and limitations, so you can apply it in other areas of your life. Here I'm focusing on it as a way to take the edge off worries about money. This becomes a shortcut to attracting more money.

This is a powerful technique, like breathing, reminding yourself that you're in the moment, and touching something physical. All these practices help bring you into the now. The now is the point of power. This is where money is. This is where your happiness is. When you come from the feeling that you already have what you want, you're better able to see your opportunities to attract more money.

## BEYOND STUCKNESS

Many people who have moneymaking ideas get stuck when it comes to implementing them. Usually being stuck has to do with a fear: the fear of failure or the fear of success. You have to look at both. Ask yourself, "If I'm truly successful with this moneymaking idea, how will I feel?" It might seem odd, but you might even want to ask, "What's the worst that could happen?" When you play out that mental scenario, you take off the charge, and you realize it's OK to be successful.

You can do the same thing with the fear of failure: if you try the moneymaking idea and it doesn't work, what's the worst that can happen? Can you survive? Will you be OK? Can you still love yourself if it's a "failure?" We'll put "failure" in quotations because we all know failure is feedback. Very often when you attempt a business idea, it gives you an education about how to perfect the idea or how to carry out a completely different idea. Until you take action and get feedback, you don't know what to do next. My first suggestion is to take off the edge—take off the fear of success or the fear of failure.

The second suggestion is to break the process down into manageable steps. If you do feel stuck, it could be because you're overwhelmed. I've written a lot of books. People will often ask me, "How do you write a book?" You write it one chapter at a time, or more importantly, one page at a time. If you're thinking, "My moneymaking idea is to record a program or create a book or open a business, but I'm overwhelmed by how to do that," you may have to simply break it down into a tiny first step. Take that tiny first step. Write the title. Write the first sentence, the first page. As you do, you'll know what the next step is. As you take step after step after step, you end up accomplishing your task over time. Those are a couple of suggestions on handling being suck.

## FIND YOUR MONEYMAKING BLISS

Maybe you feels you're meant to do something in the world of business, but you're not sure what it is. You might be wondering, "How do I discover my own moneymaking bliss?"

The truth of the matter is that you probably know what your moneymaking bliss is, but you've been afraid to admit it to yourself. Once I was giving a presentation in Florida. Bob Bly, who's a famous copywriter, overheard a conversation I was having with an older gentleman, who was saying, "I don't know what my passion is. I'm sixty-some years old. I've retired. I was an accountant. I did that all of my life. I don't want to do that anymore. I do want to attract money, but I don't know what my passion is."

"What do you do for fun?" I asked.

"I have a hobby: gardening."

"You can write an information product on gardening."

The older gentleman immediately dismissed this, saying, "There are all kind of books on gardening out there."

Bob Bly, who had been overhearing all of this, leaned over and said, "You're forgetting that there's a whole world of newbies out there who don't know what you know about gardening. If you wrote something about your method of doing gardening or about beginning gardening or Gardening 101, and focused on offering it to the newbies, you would be creating an information product and making money from your hobby."

I totally agree. In case after case, I've found that everybody has some sort of experience, education, talent, hobby, or pastime. If you're looking for a new way of making or attracting money, I'd say look to what you've been secretly doing to have fun. See if it can be turned into an information product or a business. Maybe you have to have conversations with a friend who will listen to you. Maybe you need a coach. Maybe you need a Master Mind. Maybe you just need to meditate and reflect on what you enjoy doing. Usually, if you look at what you love to do, you can find your new moneymaking idea.

## HO'OPONONPONO

At some point any conversation about attracting money has to include other people. I know that at some points in my life, I've had to deal with this issue. We run into what I'll call unawakened people. We will encounter people who are still in the victimhood stage of mentality. If you listen to them, they will bring you down. This is why it's so important to read positive material (as you're doing right now). Create a Master Mind and have a support group to counteract the effect of water cooler gossipers, whom you may have to work with, at least for a while.

What I've noticed about unawakened people is that if you ignore them, they tend to go away. I've also noticed that they tend to drop away as you work on yourself, because as you change, they're no longer attracted into your life.

As you keep working on awakening yourself, moving from victimhood to empowerment and even beyond, you remove the reason to have them in your life. In many ways, those people are simply mirroring beliefs that are within you. As you release those beliefs, those people disappear.

This is a magical universe. As you change yourself, the outer world seems to redecorate itself, repopulate itself, and completely change, so it looks as if you're now on a whole different planet.

There's a wonderful way to clear up some of the hidden beliefs within you that might be attracting some of the naysayers, some of the unawakened people in your life.

This is one of the most powerful stories I've ever heard. Years ago I heard about a therapist who worked at a mental hospital for the criminally insane in Hawaii. This hospital was a hellish place to be. Doctors would not stay. The staff would keep quitting. Turnover was horrible. The prisoners themselves, the patients were so violent that if you visited the ward, you would have to walk down with your back against the wall so that you weren't attacked. These mentally ill criminals had to be sedated or shackled every day.

Finally, the hospital hired one particular therapist. He knew what he was getting into, and he put out a demand. He said, "I will go to this hospital, but I will not see patients directly. I will use my own form of spiritual healing, and I will work on myself while I'm there."

Because the hospital was so desperate, they allowed him to come and do his particular work the way he wanted to do it.

The therapist would go into his office and close the door. He would look at the records, the charts of these different patients. As he looked at them, he would feel whatever he was feeling. It might be rage. It might be disappointment. It might be shame. It might be anger. It might be frustration. Whatever he felt, he did not try to go out and change the patients, which is what most people would do. He looked at what he was feeling. He then addressed the divine in a prayerful way and just said four phrases. The four phrases that he said were designed not to change anybody else, but to cleanse him.

When I first heard this story, I thought, "This sounds preposterous. I know about distance healing. I know about different modalities of change and transformation, but how can a therapist try to heal mentally ill criminals by not even seeing them, but only by looking at their records and talking to the divine?" It didn't make sense.

The story became even more hypnotic, because it turned out that when the therapist did this simple process on himself only, patients started to get better within weeks. Within months, some of them were no longer sedated or shackled and were even being released. Within a year, much of the staff found it fun to go to work and would stay. Other therapists wanted to be there. The whole atmosphere changed. Patients were getting better and better and were being released. After two years, almost every inmate was released. After four years, the ward was closed.

Now this is miraculous, historic, mind-bending. This therapist, instead of changing all the people around him, only worked on himself. I went and found the therapist. His name is Dr. Ihaleakala Hew Len. The method he used is called *ho'oponopono*. Dr. Hew Len would turn his eyes to the divine, and he would say these four phrases: "I love you. I'm sorry. Please forgive me. Thank you."

Those were the four phrases. Dr. Hew Len said them in whatever order he felt like at the time. He usually said them silently, but sometimes he said them out loud. He said them constantly, nonstop. Whenever something showed up within him as a response to what he saw in other people, he didn't try to change the other people. He said these four phrases.

How does this work? First, the therapist is taking complete responsibility for everything in his life. He knows that the statement, "You create your own reality," is true. It actually means something more than you may have considered. If you create your own reality, and a coworker is showing up in your life that's giving you a hard time about your new beliefs, then you've created that coworker too. You create your own reality, but your reality is everything and everybody in it. There are no exceptions to what you have created. If you create your own reality and somebody shows up that you don't like, they're in your reality, and you've created it.

Dr. Hew Len decided that he was 100 percent responsible for everything in his life, including mentally ill criminals. Changing from the outer wasn't working, so he decided that the only way to change them was to change himself. Because he didn't know all the unconscious programming that was going on within him and attracting these patients to him, he had to turn it over to a higher power. He could not do it from his ego. He could not do it from his psychological training. He had to do it through the divine. He would sit in his chair, look at those records, feel what he was feeling, address his petition to the divine, and say, "I love you, I'm sorry, please forgive me, and thank you."

You can say these phrases to remove anything that you don't like in the outer world, but more importantly, to remove all the blocks within you.

I want you to understand what you're really communicating when you say these four phrases. When you say, "I'm sorry," you're basically saying, "I'm sorry for my unconsciousness. I've had no idea, no clue, what part of me or my belief system or of my unconscious manifested and attracted whatever it is that's in my life that I don't like. I don't know where it came from, so I'm sorry I've been unaware."

"Please forgive me" is an extension of that statement. You're saying, "Please forgive me for not being conscious, for not correcting this earlier. Please forgive me for any action or inaction I may have taken or not taken in attracting or not attracting money. Please forgive me for my unconsciousness, for being unawake."

With "Thank you," you're saying, "Thank you for taking care of this. Thank you for my life. Thank you for resolving this. Thank you for cleansing and clearing the problem that I perceived in others but that's really in me." "Thank you" is the statement of gratitude.

The words "I love you," to me, are the most powerful words you can say. When you say, "I love you," you begin to reconnect with the divine itself. If you want prosperity, if you want money, if you want abundance, reconnect with the divine, because the divine *is* prosperity and abundance. When you say, "I love you," you start to merge with the essence of the divine, which is love. By addressing the divine with four statements, you're actually cleansing yourself.

This is one of the most powerful clearing methods I know of. If you're looking for a shortcut to attracting money, here it is. Get into the moment and say, "I love you. I'm sorry. Please forgive me. Thank you."

These days I say these phrases almost all the time. I want to clear anything in me that might prevent money from coming to you. After all, I created you too in my own life. I'm removing any blocks within me so that you and I both can attract more money.

Expect miracles. Expect money. Expect happiness. Expect to be in this moment, connecting with the divine.

# SIX
# MONEY MASTERY

I n this chapter, I'm going to talk about money mastery. I'm going to give you tips, insights, and resources to help you attract money at a turbocharged rate.

## MAKE WEALTH A STUDY

Let's begin with making wealth a study. You can attract more money into your life by focusing on how other people have done it. Learn from their techniques. Learn from their biographies. Learn from their secrets. You can apply them too. You can shorten your learning curve by reading and listening to other authors and incorporating this wealth study into your lifestyle.

I have a list of books and resources that I want to give you, and I believe they will help you. (Follow your intuition with all of these recommendations.) One is *Spiritual Economics* by Eric Butterworth. *Spiritual Economics* changed my life at one point many decades ago, when I was still learning how to attract money. *Spiritual Economics* is one of those wake-up call books. It's still on the shelves. Eric Butterworth has written a lot of other books, all worth reading, but I would get that one.

A couple that have written several books are Jerry and Esther Hicks. One I would recommend is *Ask and It Is Given.*

Another book that will help you understand your programming, your scripting, and your own unconscious mind is a book by Michael Ryce called *Why Is This Happening To Me . . . Again?!* It's probably one of the top five books that caused me to wake up to my own programming. Again, I think life is a process of awakening. With the book you're reading, you're awakening to how to attract money, but Michael Ryce's will help you in all areas of life, not just financially.

I also think you should be reading books by or about entrepreneur Richard Branson and books by Dan Kennedy. Dan Kennedy is a marketing genius, a marketing wizard, and he has a whole series of *No B.S.* guides that can help you think more prosperously and more like an entrepreneur.

The first book to change my life was *The Magic of Believing* by Claude Bristol. It came out in the fifties, but it has stood its test of time. It's considered to be a classic and is still in print today. I've read it maybe a dozen times, and I encourage you to read it. It says that when you believe something, you will tend to attract it into your life. Of course, this ties into everything I've been talking about, because when you believe or expect to attract money, you will find ways to do so.

*How To Get Rich,* by Felix Dennis, is well worth reading. If I can give a plug to one of my own books, I could mention my biography of P. T. Barnum, *There's a Customer Born Every Minute.* It reveals ten time-tested techniques for marketing and promoting any business. Reading it will enable you to have more of an entrepreneurial mindset.

Another wake-up call to help you understand your wealth mentality is a book by Darel Rutherford called *So, Why Aren't You Rich?* It's going to make you a little squeamish, because it gets in your face and asks you how you're thinking and acting when it comes to attracting enough money to be wealthy.

If you haven't read Napoleon Hill's classic *Think and Grow Rich,* now is the time to do it. That book has single-handedly helped more people become wealthy than possibly any other book in history. It's everywhere. You can get it in book form or on audio. Find it, read it, and reread it.

Another book that helped me was Catherine Ponder's *The Dynamic Laws of Prosperity*. It's a great companion to this book and talks about the inside spiritual and psychological approach to attracting more money.

I've already mentioned Gene Landrum's *The Superman Syndrome*. Gene Landrum has written many books, and I encourage you to read all of them. *The Superman Syndrome* is about pretending you are Superman or any billionaire or millionaire that you admire, then calling forth their traits from within you.

There are several audio programs that I also recommend, many of them from Nightingale Conant. Its website, www.nightingale.com, is a Christmas catalog of possibilities. It has numerous audios in all kinds of categories from the spiritual to self-help to the mind improvement to health and wellness. I have two audio programs with them, one called *The Missing Secret,* which explains how to use the law of attraction to pull into your life the things you want—not just money, but relationships or health or anything else that you can name. I have another program with them called *The Power of Outrageous Marketing.* If you're interested in thinking like an entrepreneur and learning marketing, publicity, and advertising techniques, get *The Power of Outrageous Marketing.*

Another program that I love is called *The Wealth Magnet* by Dr. Dolf de Roos. *The Wealth Magnet* is fantastic. I've listened to it several times. He's teaching you to change your beliefs, much as I've been teaching in this book. He's telling you that when you change your beliefs and take different actions, you start to attract more wealth.

Another program that I highly recommend is called *The Transforming Debt into Wealth System,* by John Cummuta. It's a wonderful resource to help you get out of debt and build wealth.

Another audio program that I highly recommend is called *Change Your Beliefs, Change Your Life* by Nick Hall. It includes a seven-step belief challenge process. Because we live in a belief-created universe, if you change your beliefs, you change your reality. Nick Hall's program can help you do that.

Another program I love is *Your Inner Awakening* by Byron Katie. I'm a big fan of Byron's; I've read all of her books and listened to her material. It helps me to awaken.

Finally, speaking of awakening, listen to my own program *The Awakening Course*, which describes the four stages of awakening. You can read about it at The AwakeningCourse.com or go to AwakeningDownload .com, where you can download it directly to your iPod or computer and listen to it at your leisure.

All these resources can help you attract more money. They're probably available for you at the library if you can't afford them right now. Thank God for the libraries. Go to the library. Borrow books and audios like the ones I've mentioned. When you can afford them, buy them for yourself and read and listen to them repeatedly. By doing this, you're reprogramming your mind. You're leaving victimhood and becoming empowered. You're starting to think like a wealthy person. The more you can do that, the more you will attract money.

## A NEW DEFINITION OF MARKETING

From time to time, I've run into people who have said that selling and marketing were unpleasant to them. I think a lot of that has to do with their attitude towards money in general, because if they feel good about money, they should be fine about marketing and selling, which is a tool to bring in more money.

In any event, let me give you my new definition of marketing: it's simply sharing your love for your product or service with the target audience that's going to welcome hearing about it. Most people who complain about marketing and selling do so because the message has been a mismatch: they were telling the wrong audience about their product, and of course that audience complained. When they heard about it, they felt bad.

Sometimes people try to tell something they don't believe in. Their heart isn't behind it, their love isn't behind it, their passion isn't behind it, so it feels like work. If you share your passion or love for your product or service with the people who are going to thank you for telling them about it, you have a wonderful win-win that makes the world work. You will attract money easily and effortlessly because you are serving people. They will feel it. They will feel the love, and that love will cause an abundance that you've never before imagined.

Marketing and selling are not manipulation. Marketing and selling are not hard work. Marketing and selling are not evil. Marketing and selling are sharing your love for your product or service, your business, with the right people, who are going to congratulate you, thank you, and maybe even hug you as they give you money for your product or service. Take that new definition into your heart, and you will attract more money easily and effortlessly and faster than ever before.

## TIME MANAGEMENT

Time management is part of learning to master money. Here's how I do it. Before I go to bed at night, I'll make a list of what I want to do the next day. It helps get these things off my conscious mind so I can go to sleep without thinking about my to-do list for the next day. But something deeper and more magical happens as well. I'm enlisting the help of my subconscious mind. I'm saying, "I want to work on these projects tomorrow, and you"—meaning my subconscious mind—"begin working on them now, while I'm going to sleep."

During the night, while my conscious mind is dozing off, my unconscious mind, which never goes to sleep, is working on those to-dos. The next morning when I get up and I take a look at the to-dos, I see that some of them are already done, meaning that the solutions have been formed in my mind. All I have to do is act on them, write them down, or spell them out.

For example, the night before I have a sales letter to write or an email to send out to my list, I might jot down that I want to write this communication to promote one of my works, and I would love for it to get a 95 percent response. Here I'm stating an intention, which, as you understand, is part of the five-step formula of the attractor factor. I've given a command to my unconscious mind; I've turned it over; I then go to sleep. I don't worry about the project. I trust that my mind's working on it.

The next day, when I get up, I may or may not have an idea of what to write at that point, but I go to my computer and start writing. More often than not, the material comes to me easily and effortlessly, because my unconscious mind has already worked on it before I got to the keyboard. This is one of my time management tricks: I get my subconscious mind to work for me.

Let me give you another advanced time management exercise. When I make my personal to-do list, I also have a to-do list for the universe. This might seem strange, but it works.

I make two to-do lists. One says, "Tomorrow morning at 1:00, I have an appointment. I have a phone call. I'm going to be on that call." Or I'm going to write a sales letter. Or I'm going to work out in the morning, as I usually do. It might mean that I have a business meeting. These are things for me to do physically. I'm putting them on the to-do list as a reminder and as a way to get them off my mind and start my subconscious mind working on them.

The second to-do list is composed of the things I want the universe to do for me. For example, if I have a new book and I want to sell it to a big publisher, I might put on the list, "Universe, please lead the publisher to me, or lead me to the publisher to help me get the best deal for this new book." I'm stating an intention for the universe. I'm sending a message in a bottle, so to speak, out into the ethers. The universe will then pick up this message and vibrationally match the solution to me. Along the way, I'll get a phone call, or I'll see an ad in a magazine or an article in the newspaper, or I will overhear a conversation that will lead me to the publisher I was looking for.

With this process, I'm enlisting the help of my subconscious mind, and I'm enlisting the help of the universe itself.

## GETTING A LOT DONE

People often ask me, "How do you get so much done? What do you work on first?"

I work first on the thing that has the most energy in it. I look at my to-dos for the day and say, "Which one is calling me? Which one has the most energy on it? Which one is saying, 'I'm first'?" Whatever that is, I do first.

When it comes to hour by hour ways of managing your time, my rule of thumb is, if there's something that's unpleasant on my list, something I'm not looking forward to doing—my taxes for example—I will either do it first to get it over with (then I can reward myself with something that's much more fun), or find somebody who thinks it's fun and hire them to do it.

This might be one of the most important time management secrets you've ever heard: I used to do my taxes myself. I did not like it; I did not understand it; I was not good at it; I probably made a lot of mistakes at it. It used up my time and energy. When I finally said, "This is not fun for me," and I found somebody who regarded it as fun and paid them to do it, my income multiplied ten times.

This is an important money attraction secret. If you do what's fun for you, you keep your energy up. You keep your energy soaring. You keep moving forward. Because your energy is up, the vibration that you send out into the universe causes you to bring in more wealth and more high vibration opportunities.

When you do things that you don't enjoy, you are causing your energy to drop. When your energy drops, you don't feel good. You aren't happy. You send out a signal that causes new experiences to come in to match the low energy. It's a spiral down. If you want to spiral up, start giving other people things to do, especially if you don't enjoy them.

This is one of the greatest time and project management secrets that I've ever come up with. In short, do what's fun for you, and you will attract more money into your life.

## WHAT BUSINESS DO I OPEN?

Let's talk about the attractor factor system for attracting money and tailor it to something specific for you. You've gotten through this book up to this point, and you're wondering, "What business do I open? What do I do as an entrepreneur? How do I think like an entrepreneur? What do I do next? How do I bring money in when I'm still feeling broke?" Maybe you're buying a whole lot of what I've been talking about and taking action on some of my suggestions. You're sitting there now, saying, "What do I do next?"

Let's use the five-step formula on that. The first step is to know what you *don't* want. If you're sitting there saying, "I don't know what to do next," perfect. That's what the first step has brought to you.

Change that complaint into the second step: select what you do want. What's your intention? If you don't know what to do next, your intention is probably something like, "I want to know with absolute clarity what the next move is for me," "I want to know with absolute clarity how to attract more money into my life right now," "I want to know with absolute clarity how to open a business or what business to open," or "I want to know with absolute clarity the right way for me to go into business and start attracting more money." Somewhere in there is your intention.

Step number three is to get clear of the interference between you and your intention. If you're starting to think, "I don't know what I'm going to do; I don't believe all of this is going to work; I still feel poor," this is where you have to use some of the techniques I've been discussing to investigate your beliefs. One of the simplest is ho'oponopono, which I discussed in the last chapter.

You are feeling your frustration. You are feeling your indecision. You don't know where it's coming from. You don't know how to remove it, but you address your concern to the divine, whatever that means to you. You say, "I'm sorry. Please forgive me. Thank you. I love you." You're saying, "I'm sorry. I don't know how I created this state of indecision and confusion. I don't know how I created this experience of feeling poor. Please forgive me for whatever I thought, whatever my grandparents thought, whatever is in my DNA, whatever is in my system that causes me to feel this way. Please forgive me for it, because I did not know and they did not know what they were doing."

"Thank you" means, "Thank you for erasing this. Thank you for clarifying this. Thank you for clearing this. Thank you for getting me back to a place of peace in this moment."

"I love you" is the most powerful statement to reconnect you to the experience of the divine, which for me is nothing but love. You can get clear by going through the ho'oponopono process.

The fourth step in our million-dollar secret formula is to feel what it would be like to already have, do, or be what you want. In this case, because you want to know what to do next in your life or what to do next to attract more money, what would it feel like if you had the money? What would it feel like if you knew what to do next right now?

Just imagine this for a moment. Mentally allow yourself to already be there: now you know what to do next. What does that feel like, even without knowing what to do next? What does it feel like in your body? How does it feel in your mind? How does your energy feel when you pretend that you already know? If you're trying to attract more money now, what does it feel like to already have the money? You've got the money. There's a big pile of cash in your lap right now. Suddenly you look at your bank account, and it's swollen. Some miracle took place, and there's more money there than you ever imagined before. How did that happen? Who cares? It happened. What does that feel like?

That's the fourth step: imagine that the intention has come to pass right now.

Finally, let go of your addiction or attachment, your need to have anything work out in a particular way. You let go of your anxiety. You remind yourself, "I'm OK. I'm in this moment, and all is well. I don't need to worry. I don't need to fret. Everything is unfolding in a divine order. Maybe I don't see the whole picture, but I trust the unfolding." It's a flower that's blooming, and the flower is you.

As you feel these things, you may be getting nudges to do something. Maybe it's to go to the Small Business Administration. Maybe it's to answer an ad, send out a résumé, open a business, or watch a particular business TV show. I don't know what it'll be, but it will bubble up from within you as a direct result of this million-dollar secret formula.

Follow these steps. Do them mentally, and do them in writing. They will guide you in what to do next, what to decide next, and how to feel abundant right now.

## STRIPPED DOWN GUITAR

If you've been sitting there wondering where to begin your business, or if you've been struggling with an idea for a product or service, and you just can't quite seem to see it, I've got good news. It's selling information. This is really huge, especially on the Internet, a place where I've been specializing in selling information products for decades.

It's very simple. Look at your own passions, your hobbies, your experience, your education to find out what you've been doing that other people would be interested in knowing how to do themselves. Once you put this down in writing, you can sell that information to them. Hear me out, because this is fascinating and really juicy. It's a great moneymaking opportunity for anybody, including you.

Once a woman came to visit me when I was living in Austin, Texas. She had heard about the Internet; she had heard about me. She really couldn't believe that you could make money online.

We had lunch. I answered all of her questions, but she was very skeptical. She kept saying that she didn't see where she could make any money online; she was only in her twenties. She had no real experience, no real education, no unique background, so how could she make any sort of information product to sell on the Internet?

I listened to her, and I asked a few questions. I said, "What do you like to do?"

She liked to go biking.

"What are you interested in?"

"I'm interested in raw foods."

"What is your passion? What are your experiences? What have you done for hobbies?"

"Well, I taught myself to play the guitar."

She probably could have done a raw foods cookbook. She might have done something on biking, maybe the secret biking trails of Texas or the Austin area. But when I heard that she taught herself how to play the guitar, my ears perked up, and I thought, "Now that sounds interesting." I asked her, "How did you teach yourself how to play the guitar?"

"I taught myself to play it in one weekend."

"Wait a minute. You taught yourself how to play the guitar in one weekend?"

"Yes. It's just my own method. I taught myself to play the guitar because I wanted to play a few songs, and now I can play the guitar. I started in one weekend."

"Have you ever taught this to anybody else?"

"No. There are lots of guitar instruction books out there."

"That doesn't matter," I said. "People always want to learn new things. If there's an audience for a particular service or product or hobby, there's a built-in demand for more information in that category."

I love guitars. I collect guitars. I'm always learning how to play the guitar and wanting to learn faster ways to learn it. I'm not much different from the audience who would want to learn how to play it in one weekend. I urged her to write down her method. She was a little resistant, but she trusted me. She looked at my lifestyle and my name on the Internet. She thought, "I guess this Joe Vitale knows how to make money online. I'll listen to him."

She wrote up a little e-book, which she called *Stripped Down Guitar*. In it she explained how she taught herself how to play the guitar in one weekend, and she walked people through how to play the guitar themselves. I read it and loved it. I thought it was very simple. It was very conversational. The book was not very long, and that's the wonder of e-books or digital products or information products: they don't have to be very detailed. Get to the point. Teach people what you promised to teach them, and stop.

I told the woman to add a few photographs to the book, because it would help people visualize what she was explaining. Then I told her to turn her Microsoft Word document into a PDF document, which almost every computer can read. She turned her book into a PDF and showed it to me.

I said, "This is an information product." I told her how to put up a website. She put up the website by going to GoDaddy.com and buying the domain for Stripped DownGuitar.com. Then she paid to have a website put up to sell the e-book. I then told her to go to ClickBank. ClickBank.com is a place where people can buy your particular product. ClickBank will process the credit cards and send you a check every couple weeks. I explained all this to her.

Then I told her, "Let's tell the world about your e-book." She began to market and promote it. I told my list about it, so she immediately started to get some sales. She knew to go online and Google groups. She typed in "guitar instruction" or "guitar classes" or "guitar groups," and Google would bring back to her all the different places where people were interested in guitar instruction and guitar playing. She would go to those different groups and mention that she had come out with this e-book. I don't remember what she charged for it. It might have been $19.95 or $25.95. She began to make thousands of dollars a day.

The punch line comes along because somebody who bought that book went to her and said, "I love your book so much, I want to buy the rights to distribute it myself." She sold the rights to her e-book for $10,000.

This is pretty remarkable when you consider that when the young lady first came to me, she had no idea what to write about. She had no clue how to make a PDF or an e-book. She had no idea what ClickBank was or GoDaddy. She had no idea that she could personally make money from something she was doing as a pastime or a passion for herself. She was broke when she first came to me. She admitted that she was borrowing from her parents in order to pay her bills. She went from zero to making thousands of dollars a day to making a $10,000 payday.

I don't know how much $10,000 means to you, but it means a lot to me, and it meant a lot to her. It was like winning the lottery. That's what happens when you start creating information products. You actually create products that sell while you sleep.

The first time I had this happen was some decades ago, when I created an information product called *Hypnotic Writing*. It's now out there as a published book, and I still think you can get it as an e-book. The first time we released it as an e-book, I think we charged $29.95 for it. You can charge whatever you want for an e-book, because it's information, and people are paying to get the solution. They don't care how big it is or how fancy it is; they just want the problem solved.

In this case, readers wanted to learn how to write hypnotically (a concept I created). I announced *Hypnotic Writing*, sold it for $29.95, and overnight, I sold six hundred copies of it.

Understand that an e-book is not a printed book. It's something you read on your computer. It's a digital file, sometimes a text file, usually a PDF file, which means there's nothing to print, warehouse, or ship. This is, in many ways, an invisible product, but it's very real to the person buying it.

Something else that's wonderful happens here—instantaneous gratification. You instantly get the customer's money, and the customer instantly gets the product. It all happens in real time. When I came out with *Hypnotic Writing*, I saw that this was a powerful, wonderful way to attract money into my life. I then came out with many other e-books, including *Hypnotic Selling Stories*, *The Hypnotic Swipe File*, and a whole long series of hypnotic this and that books to go with my brand, which at that point in history was me.

This is not unusual. In case you're skeptical, thinking, "I don't have any passions; I don't have any interests; I don't have any hobbies," you don't even need to have any of that. You can release a public domain book. A public domain book is a book that has fallen out of copyright. Generally speaking, if a book was published before 1925, it's probably in the public domain, which means anybody in the public can reissue that book.

Let me give you an example of how wonderful this can be. A few years ago, I came across a series of books on

Pelmanism. Pelmanism was created at the Pelman Institute for the Scientific Development of Mind, Memory, and Personality in London in the 1920s. It's all about self-help and spirituality. I read and loved it. I thought, "Somebody needs to bring this back to the world." Why not me? I turned all of those books into e-books. I scanned every page. You can also even type out every page and turn it into a Word document, and then turn it into a PDF document so any computer can read it.

I turned Pelmanism into an online information course. I then did something that everybody else thought was genius, although to me it was just the logical next thing to do.

Since Pelmanism came out in the 1920s, I wondered if I could find the ads that were used to sell the course back then. I went poking around. Google is such a wonderful search tool that I quickly found some full-page ads for the Pelmanism course. These ads came out in the 1920s, so they were also in the public domain. I put up a website with my friend Pat O'Bryan. We drove people to the Pelmanism site.

Here's the good news. That's a course I did not write. That's an ad I did not write. It was all in the public domain. I found this material, turned it into a digital product, and put it online. Pelmanism became one of my all-time best sellers. We sold tens of thousands of copies. People would go to the website. They would read the ad for Pelmanism, they would buy it, and Pat O'Bryan and I would split the money that came in.

Even if you're thinking, "I don't have a product; I don't have a service," if you do some research, you can find something.

Here's a tip: when you start looking for a public domain product, see if you can find one in your area of interest. I really believe following your passion is one of the most powerful ways to attract more money in your life. If you're passionate about guitars, search for a public domain book on guitars, maybe from the 1800s. If you're interested in magic tricks, there are many books in the public domain from the 1800s on magic and conjuring. If you're interested in dolls or sewing or cooking or healing or whatever it happens to be, you can search for public domain books in any of those categories by using Google or the site called Gutenberg.com. You can find an information product that you didn't even write.

Here's another tip to elevate your thinking even higher. When you find something in the public domain, you can make it more your product by commenting on it. The book *The Science of Getting Rich* by Wallace Wattles was published in 1910, so it's in the public domain. Because it inspired the movie *The Secret*, a lot of people have republished it. You can find various editions of it in any bookstore right now.

One day I walked into a bookstore, and there was an edition of *The Science of Getting Rich* by Wallace Wattles and another person. This other person reprinted it with his own commentary. This makes the book unique and much more valuable, and truthfully gives you a product of your own.

You can take this idea and run with it: P. T. Barnum, who, as I've said, was a marketing genius, delivered a talk that was later transcribed and published as a book called *The Art of Money Getting*. It's been reprinted a few times. Because it's in the public domain (Barnum died in 1891), I could release an edition that would say, "*The Art of Money Getting*, by P. T. Barnum and Dr. Joe Vitale." Wherever Barnum talked about one of his tips or insights, I could update it with a story, a news item, a comment of my own. I would end up creating a whole new information product. I'd be a coauthor with the great P. T. Barnum.

Another example: there's a public domain book called *Thought Vibration* by Walter Atkinson, first published in 1906. It is a wonderful book. I love it; it's very readable. If I wanted to use this strategy, I might take *Thought Vibration* and comment on it, expand on some of the things the author said, and include my thoughts. Then it becomes *Thought Vibration* by Walter Atkinson and Dr. Joe Vitale.

You can do this too. You can do any or all of these things. I've just given you a course in creating your own information empire by paying attention to your passions, interests, skills, and hobbies, and even going beyond that to finding public domain works that you can republish and recreate. You can go further still to coauthoring with a dead author on a public domain work into which you breathe new life. These are powerful, exciting ways to passionately attract more money.

## DRAWING TRAFFIC

At this point, you may be wondering, how do you get traffic to your website? How do you get those eyeballs on your web page so that people can read your sales letter, buy your product, and send you money?

Right now I'm going to tell you three ways to bring traffic. They work all the time.

The first one involves a freebie. My friend Pat O'Bryan was struggling and in debt; he wanted to attract money but didn't know how. After learning the principles you've been learning here, he went on to create his own Internet empire.

When Pat first came to me, he had created an e-book called the *Think and Grow Rich Workbook*. He loved *Think and Grow Rich*, but the book, first published in 1938, was lengthy and wordy. It was hard to read, hard to follow, and hard to understand. It needed a workbook, so Pat created one.

This workbook was a genius idea; it was very inspired. It consisted of pages with many questions and lots of space to write your answers. Pat did not reprint *Think and Grow Rich*. Instead he just said, "You just read chapter 1 of *Think and Grow Rich*. What were the key points in it?" and gave you some space to write down your answers.

I loved the concept. I thought it was a useful study tool. I think workbooks are genius. Pat came to me and said, "I want to sell the *Think and Grow Rich Workbook*. Will you promote it to your list?"

"No," I said. "I don't think that's the right thing to do. You're just starting out. You need your own email list. It would be wiser thing to give the book away.

"Now," I explained to him, "you don't just give the book away for nothing. You give it away in exchange for a person's name and email address."

See how this works. I would then tell my list, or anybody would tell their list, that I'd just found a remarkable new information product called the *Think and Grow Rich Workbook*. It's yours free. All you have to do is go to Pat's website. There you give your email address, and he will give you the workbook.

This is how Pat developed a mailing list of his own from nothing, zero, to six hundred to six thousand names in a few days. It's probably still growing.

Pat was able to seed the beginning of his empire by giving something away. I've talked about karmic marketing before. I want to remind you that when you give now, you will receive later. You just have to give with an open, expectant heart.

Pat decided giving away his e-book was a wise strategy for building a mailing list. This is one way to build traffic for your website. Give something away. It may be wise to give away the first information product you create.

I know at first you're going to hesitate, because you want to make money. Pat was the same way. He paused and thought, "No, I want to sell the book. I actually want to make money from the *Think and Grow Rich Workbook*." But he trusted me and said, "I will try your particular strategy. I'll try your method."

He's very glad he did, because once he had his own email list, he was able to go to that list repeatedly whenever he came out with a new product. He didn't have to worry about building traffic at that point, because he had traffic parked on his own list. He came out with around forty products in the next year. Every time he did, he told his list. He began by building traffic by giving something away.

The second step in creating traffic is to tell owners of other relevant lists about your product. This ties into the first step, because Pat came to me. I'm a list owner; I have a list of tens of thousands of names; I actually have several mailing lists. Pat knew that, so he came to me and said, "Joe, if you tell your list about my *Think and Grow*

*Rich Workbook*, they will love the book. They will get it for free, and you, Joe, will look like a hero because you found this wonderful news bulletin and freebie for your list."

That's what you do. You Google other list owners. You might come out with a guitar product, a skiing product, a fitness product of some sort, a musical product, a gardening product—you can come up with so many different things that it's staggering. The opportunities are basically infinite.

You would Google the topic, looking for list owners. You're looking for websites that come up when you do your Google search. When you find a list owner for your product, you write to them and say, "I have this product. Would you be interested in selling it to your list?"

Now if you've done like Pat O'Bryan, you might give this away in order to build your own list. I think that's a brilliant strategy.

If you really want to make money doing this at the first stage, you tell the list owner that your product is listed on ClickBank. This means that they can be an affiliate for your product. An affiliate is like a commissioned salesperson. Whenever an affiliate sells your product, they get a portion of the sale. If your product sells for $30 and you have set an affiliate commission of, say, 50 percent (though that's a little high), every time somebody bought through that list owner, the owner would make $15, and you would make $15. This is why a list owner will promote your product to their list. There's something in it for them.

The second way to drive traffic toward your site, then, is find list owners and tell them about your product. Of course you want to find relevant list owners. If you have a product for babies, you don't want to offer it to a list for senior citizens.

The third way to send traffic to your website is to tell news groups. Just as there are lists for every subject or niche that you can think of, there are groups. Again, you'll go to the wonderful tool Google, click on it, and search for groups. You would search for "guitar news groups" or "guitar forums."

Let me give you a bonus tip. Another way to drive traffic to your website is to send out a news release. Far too many people fail to do this. The media is starving for good stories. When you tell them that you have a product or service, you're giving them a potential story they can run with. I'm a big fan of doing this; I have been doing it my entire career. It's one of my own personal secrets to success. Send out a news release.

There's a couple of ways to send out a news release. First of all, a news release is nothing but a single sheet of paper. It is not very detailed. It's not an entire article. It's the basic who, what, when, where, and how. You're basically giving the reporter a news bulletin. You're signaling to him that there is possibly a story here; take a look at it.

You send out the news release in a couple of different ways. One of my favorites is online. You can Google "news release distribution services," and several will come up: PRWeb.com, NewsDirect.com, iMediaFacts.com are all places where you can send out news releases. Many of them have examples of news releases. They have advisors on staff that can review your news release. That's one way.

The other way—and this is a seldom used, rarely known trick—is to get the media directory from your local Chamber of Commerce. Every Chamber of Commerce in every big city has one. If you're in a small city, go to the next biggest city and ask its Chamber of Commerce for its media directory. The directory will cost anywhere from $15 to $50, rarely more. It will list every news station, TV, radio station, news bulletin, syndicate service, wire service, Internet bulletin service, website. You then send your news release wherever it appears to be relevant. When they run your story, they will be driving traffic to your website. Why would they do that? Because it's a service to their readers.

## A BUSINESS PURPOSE EXERCISE

To bring all this together, let's do a business purpose exercise. You probably want to do this when you are at home, when you are relaxed. You're in a comfortable chair. The phone's off. You're not checking email.

Nobody's going to disturb you. You can focus on your heart and your purpose.

Say you are relaxing in a comfortable chair. You're taking in a few deep breaths and slowly letting them go. You're relaxing. Nowhere else to go. Nothing else to do. You can take it easy right now and focus on you.

Notice your breathing. Your breathing is slow and relaxed. You're following your breath in, and you're following your breath out.

As you're relaxing and letting your mind settle, think about your five favorite things to do. They could be five hobbies or pastimes. They can be five things that you end up doing every day or week. Just let them bubble up into your mind, with no criticism or judgment. Welcome any image, any word, any thought. You might write them down, or you might just let them float around in your consciousness.

As these five or six things come to mind, notice if one of them seems more playful, more exciting, more energetic than the others. Whatever that one is, let it come to the top of the list. Let it come to the top of your mind. If you have two things that seem to be coming in with the same power and energy, let them both come to the top of your awareness.

I invite you to consider, is there a business in one or two of those hobbies or pastimes that have come to your mind? Can you imagine turning those items into an information product—something that would help other people understand that hobby or passion? You might even get creative and imagine combining one, two, or three more from your list. What if you combine the first item with the second? What if you combine the first item with the fifth? This is a wonderful way to stretch your mind and come up with something completely new and creative, something that may never have been done before.

Again, don't judge this process. Allow your ideas to come up. When you feel like it, you can write them down, or just sit with them and see how you might develop them. For example, the woman who had no clue of what to do to make money remembered that she taught herself how to play the guitar in one weekend. It ended up attracting a great deal of money to her. Maybe you have a hobby that other people can learn from. You don't have to be a master of that hobby. All you have to do is be conversant with it. Maybe you have a slight angle, a new twist to the hobby. Maybe you have tied that first hobby to a second or third hobby and created a new way of doing either one of them, or maybe you created an entirely new hobby. It doesn't matter. Right now, you're just allowing yourself to accept new possibilities.

Now let these things float out of your awareness for a moment. Begin to play with the possibility that you have more money than you could ever spend. What would it feel like to be in a place where you have bought all the houses you want, all the cars you want, all the clothes you want? You have taken all the trips you want. You're now sitting here, relaxing, feeling wonderful. You've donated money to good causes. You've built what you've wanted. You've bought the toys you wanted. You've paid all the bills. You are free and financially clear to do whatever you want. What are you going to do next? What would be fun for you to do? When you have all bills paid and money is unlimited, pouring in at a rate that you will never be able to spend, what will you do businesswise? Will you open up a particular business? Will you do something that's connected to one of the hobbies that were in your mind a moment ago? What would you do if you weren't concerned about making money?

You might want to make note of your answer mentally and write it down later. For a few moments, I want you to install in your mind the feeling that all bills are paid for, all money is coming to you easily and effortlessly, you can never outspend it, you have everything you want, you can do whatever you want. You can do something worthwhile in your business and your life, and you will always succeed.

How does that feel? Feel it in your body right now. Maybe anchor this wonderful feeling by touching your thumb and forefinger together for just a minute and squeezing and releasing. Again, ask yourself, "Now that I have all the money in the world, I have attracted money beyond belief, what do I want to do to attract even more money?"

Feel this wonderful, complete feeling, integrate it in your body. Again, anchor it by touching your thumb and forefinger together and squeezing for a moment. Then release. Take a deep breath. Remind yourself of where you are in this room and this chair.

Reflect on all the answers you've just received. As quickly as you can, write them down. From this exercise, you have discovered your business purpose, your money-making idea. You are welcome to do this whenever you feel like it.

I am very excited for you. We've had quite an adventure to get to the point where you know the secret to attracting money. I don't want to end here; I want it to begin here. I have a phrase; it's my motto. It's from sixteenth-century Latin: *aude aliquid dignum.* It means, "Dare something worthy." I don't want you to just sit there and pay your bills. I want you to go beyond that. I want you to open a business. I want you to become an entrepreneur who is making more than enough money to take care of all of your bills, all of your dreams, all of your desires. I want you to help your friends, your family, your community, and your world at large. I want you to dare something worthy so that you make a difference in this world, in your life, in the planet, in everybody you touch.

I want you to do something now. I want you to get up. I want you to take action. I want you to realize that money loves speed.

You've gotten ideas. You've gotten inspiration. You've gotten tools. You've gotten techniques. You've gotten strategy. You've gotten methods from everything I've shared throughout this book. It's now up to you. You have to take action. If you sit there and do nothing, your life will be the same tomorrow. You have to take action now. Think differently. Act differently. Begin right this moment. Dare something worthy. I believe in you. I have given you everything I know about how to attract money. It's up to you to take action. As you do so, you will attract money at staggering levels.

# SEVEN
# THE TEN MOST IMPORTANT BUSINESS LESSONS

n this final chapter, I want to talk about ten of the most important business lessons I've ever learned. These are lessons that will help you attract money. They help explain the secret to attracting money in your life.

## 1. GIVE YOURSELF A BREAK

Lesson number one is to *give yourself a break*. I've been through very tough times in my life. I was homeless. I struggled. I starved. I went through long periods of unemployment and indecision. I went through long periods of feeling as if nothing was going to work out. Where was the money? Where was my job? Are things going to work out for me? When am I finally going to get published?

Because I wanted to be an author, I kept struggling, wanting, desiring to make that dream come true. At some point, I realized I had to stop and forgive myself. I had to stop and say, "Joe, you are doing the best you can." I think that's true for all of us. Maybe you struggled in the past, You might be struggling now. Whatever the case may be, give yourself a break. Forgive, let go, and grow.

This is one of the biggest lessons, because if you carry around the past, you're not going to be able to create the future you want. The energy that you're using to carry that luggage in your emotional energy system is preventing your from releasing it to attract money into your life right now. You've got to forgive and let go and grow.

## 2. HYPNOSIS

Lesson number two is about *hypnosis*. Hypnosis may be subtle, but it's a powerful tool. I am a hypnotherapist, and I've spoken at the National Guild of Hypnotists several times over the years. I have written *Hypnotic Writing* and a book called *Buying Trances*, so I know about the power of the mind. I know about the power of trance.

The thing to realize here is that all of us are in a cultural trance. We are in a trance, which is a mindset, a belief system that has been installed in us over the decades since we were growing up. We're born into the stage of feeling like a victim. We download all this information from family, friends, school systems, media, religion, government—everybody around us—about how the world works. It's not necessarily accurate. When you awaken from this victimhood mindset and move into an empowerment mindset, you start to attract more money in your life, because you start to have more power and more energy to make new decisions.

Hypnosis has helped me realize that we're all in a trance of one sort of another. If you want to be in the money-attracting trance, you have to wake up from the scarcity trance. I've done that, and you can too.

## 3. THE SMALLEST GESTURES CARRY THE GREATEST WEIGHT

Lesson number three: *the smallest gestures carry the greatest weight.* I've managed to be on Larry King twice, I was on Donny Deutsch's *Big Idea* on CNBC, then in several movies, including *The Secret*, and some of it has happened because I did little things. I was able to give somebody a book, which was then given to a producer, which was the reason for a phone call. But when I made the little gesture, it wasn't to make something happen. It came from my heart. I did something because my heart said, "Do this." I gave something because my heart said, "Give this."

This little thing caused a ripple in the universe, and it came back to me. I think this is a lesson about appreciating your own intuition, acting on your own inner nudges, and trusting that they will go somewhere profound. The little gestures you offer right now can be the lever that kicks in your ability to attract more money.

## 4. APPRECIATION

Lesson four is all about *appreciation*. I firmly believe that when you appreciate what you have, you will receive more. When you are in this moment, feeling gratitude for this moment, you up your vibrational signal to attract more things to be grateful for.

This isn't complicated. When you're in this moment and you're grateful for what's going on, you feel better. You feel lighter. You feel happier. When you appreciate anything with genuine sincerity in this moment, you begin to attract new experiences to be grateful for. What you get in the next few moments is going to be based on what you feel in this moment. Recently I read a study that said your unconscious mind does things three days out, meaning that what you feel right now is going to bring about a response three days from now.

When you're aware of this fact, you start to become acutely aware of how you think, how you believe, and how you radiate. Lesson number four is about appreciating the moment, feeling grateful right now, moving into the essence of the "be here now" moment, when nothing else matters and nothing else is possible. When you feel grateful in this moment, three days from now, or moments from now, you will have more to be grateful for. This is a powerful lesson.

## 5. LEARN FROM THE PAST

Lesson number five: *don't lean on the past; learn from it and move on.* This isn't just about letting go but about learning from the experience. I've tried many businesses, some of which didn't work out. They didn't work out the way I expected them to. When they don't work out, it might be perceived as a failure at that time. But if you see that a failure is really an opportunity to do something different, you can learn from it and move forward, adapting as you go. As you do, you end up attracting money that you never thought would show up. The past can be a great educator. Just don't get locked into it.

## 6. FIND YOUR VOICE

Lesson number six: *find your voice and speak your truth.* This is another very big lesson and a very big moneymaking opportunity for you. A long time ago, I wrote a little booklet called *Spiritual Marketing.* It was reincarnated, revised, and republished as *The Attractor Factor*, which is alive and well. It's the book that got me into *The Secret*; it's been reissued in a second edition, and it's still a best seller; it's doing great. But I all began with a little booklet called *Spiritual Marketing*.

Here's the punch line. I was afraid to release *Spiritual Marketing*. I was afraid that the world would judge me as too metaphysical. At that point I was published by the American Marketing Association and the American Management Association—very big, very conservative organizations—and I didn't want to damage my reputation by coming out with a little booklet called *Spiritual Marketing*.

Yet I did come out with it, thanks to the support of my friend Bob Proctor. That book touched a nerve in people, and hundreds of people immediately wanted it. I started giving it away as an e-book. Millions of people immediately downloaded it. Later it was published as *The Attractor Factor*, which led to a long series of successes.

At first I didn't want to release *Spiritual Marketing*; I was afraid. Here's the great lesson: when you face your fear, you often attract great wealth. This is part of finding your voice and speaking your truth. When I realized that *Spiritual Marketing* was coming directly from my heart, that this was an important part of my mission in life, I took a deep breath and said, "I will face my fears, and I will release this book." Of course I had support in releasing it. When it came out and I learned that it was becoming a best seller and *The New York Times* wrote about it, I knew that it was the right thing to do.

But many people don't act because of their fear. One of the great lessons is to face your fear, act on your desires, find your voice, and speak your truth. When you do, you unlock the vault to help you attract more money.

## 7. THE WORLD IS A WONDERFUL PLACE

Lesson number seven is realizing that *the world is a benevolent, compassionate, wonderful place.* The only reason you don't have most of the things you want is you. That is not cause for blame or guilt. It means that your financial situation is due to the unconscious programming within you.

Obviously, you have not been consciously aware of what's going on in your unconscious, so you can't blame yourself. You can't condemn yourself for where you are at this point. But you can awaken. You can awaken to realize that this world is a loving place, that the divine is trying to bless you with all of the things you wanted, even more than you ever imagined. You have to get out of the way.

I have spent decades working on myself. It's the only way I was able to go from homeless man to multimillionaire. I have consistently, relentlessly pursued my own self-development, and I'm still doing it today. You can too.

When you pause and realize that the universe wants you to succeed, that it is blessing you and loving right now, and you begin to entertain that possibility, you begin to open yourself up to change. You begin to open yourself up to receiving money.

## 8. YOU HAVE MORE POWER THAN YOU SUSPECT

Lesson number eight is an advanced lesson. It's realizing that although you don't have total control of the universe, *you have more power than you have ever suspected.*

Quite often I talk about the four stages of awakening. The first stage is victimhood. In victimhood, people do a lot of blaming; right up to their death, their life is everybody else's fault.

When something like this book comes along, you can move into empowerment. Empowerment is a much more wonderful, energizing, happy place to be.

There are two more stages after that. The third stage is to awaken to the idea that there's a higher power. I call it the *divine.* You can surrender to the divine, and you can work with it to create more in your life than you ever thought possible, including attracting more money. This is an amazing step. It's an amazing lesson. Most of us try to run our lives by our ego and we run them into the ground, but you can turn your life over to a higher power and take direction from that power. Then you can actually have a wonderful life of moment by moment awe and wonder, including attracting more money.

## 9. CREATE SPACE FOR YOURSELF

Lesson number nine is that *create space for yourself.* You have to create me time, down time, relaxation time. As I've said, almost every night I get into the hot tub and I relax. I'm under the Texas stars, I look up, and I say, "Thank you. Thank you for my life." You don't have to wait until you are in a hot tub to say this; you can start saying it now. You can start saying, "Thank you for where I'm at. Thank you for my life. Thank you for this book."

You also start making time for yourself—meditation time, R and R time. This is important. It keeps you healthy so that you can go forward and create and attract more money, more wealth, more heaven on earth.

## 10. THE GREAT MYSTERY

Finally, lesson number ten is that *there is a great mystery* that orchestrates our world. This is actually the fourth stage of awakening, when you realize you have merged and are one with the divine itself. As Shakespeare said, "All the world's a stage, / And all the men and women merely players."

You begin to dance with that mystery, and you grow in awe of it. At that point of awakening, whether you want to attract more money or not, you look around and realize your life is one of moment by moment wonderment. When you truly feel this moment by moment mystery, magic, and miracle, you begin to attract some of the things you had longed for the longest time, including more money.

These are ten of the most important lessons I've learned about attracting more money. As I look back over my life, I remember that there were moments where I did not want to take the next risk. I did not want to take the next step. I did not want to release the next book or the next project or open the next business. I didn't want to do it because I was afraid. I was afraid that it might cause me to lose money rather than make money. I was afraid that it might cause me to be embarrassed rather than successful.

I am so glad I took the risks. I am so glad that I took the next steps. It has helped me learn. It has helped me grow. It has helped me become wealthier. It has helped me get to the place where I can share these insights with you.

I'm encouraging you to do something worthy in your own life. I'm encouraging you to face those fears, to take those risks, to learn from all of the steps you take, because at the end of this road, and during the journey, is the most wonderful experiences that you will ever have or ever imagine, but you have to take the next step. It's up to you.

I'm glad I've done it. I'm in a far greater, more peaceful, more financially abundant, more joyful place in my life, and it's all available to you too. It's your turn now.

# ABOUT THE AUTHOR

Dr. Joe Vitale is a globally famous author, marketing guru, movie, TV, and radio personality, musician, and one of the top 50 inspirational speakers in the world.

His many bestselling books include *The Attractor Factor*, *Attract Money Now*, *Zero Limits*, *The Miracle: Six Steps to Enlightenment*, and *Anything Is Possible*.

He's also recorded numerous bestselling audio programs, from The Missing Secret and The Zero Point to The Power of Outrageousness Marketing and The Awakening Course.

A popular, leading expert on the law of attraction in many hit movies, including The Secret, Dr. Vitale discovered the "missing secret" not revealed in the movie. He's been on Larry King Live, Donny Deutsch's "The Big Idea,"

CNN, CNBC, CBS, ABC, Fox News: Fox & Friends and Extra TV. He's also been featured in *The New York Times* and *Newsweek*.

One of his most recent accomplishments includes being the world's first self-help singer-songwriter as seen in 2012's *Rolling Stone Magazine*. To date, he has released seventeen albums! Several of his songs were recognized and nominated for the Posi Award, regarded as "The Grammys of Positive Music."

Well-known not only as a thinker, but as a healer, clearing people's subconscious minds of limiting beliefs, Dr. Joe Vitale is also an authentic practitioner of modern Ho'oponopono, certified Reiki healer, certified Chi Kung practitioner, certified Clinical Hypnotherapist, certified NLP practitioner, Ordained Minister, and Doctor of Metaphysical Science.

He is a seeker and a learner; once homeless, he has spent the last four decades learning how to master the powers that channel the pure creative energy of life without resistance, and created the Miracles Coaching® and Zero Limits Mastery® programs to help people achieve their life's purpose. He lives in the Austin, Texas area.

His main site is www.MrFire.com.